TRUST ISSUES

Why Traditional Estate Planning
Has Failed Us And What To Do About It

BY
RICK DURFEE

The Anti Trust Fund Baby Manifesto

Why 90% of Inherited Wealth Disappears by the Grandchildren, and How to Be the Family That Breaks the Cycle

TRUST ISSUES: WHY TRADITIONAL ESTATE PLANNING HAS FAILED US AND WHAT TO DO ABOUT IT

DURFEE, RICK, Author
TRUST ISSUES.
RICK DURFEE

In association with:
ELITE ONLINE PUBLISHING
63 East 11400 South
Suite #230
Sandy, UT 84070
EliteOnlinePublishing.com

Durfee Law Group, PLLC
DurfeeLawGroup.com

ISBN: 9798293519842 (Paperback)
ISBN: 9798293520190 (Hardcover)

BUS027030
BUS050040

QUANTITY PURCHASES: Schools, companies, professional groups, clubs, and other organizations may qualify for special terms when ordering quantities of this title. For information, email info@DurfeeLawGroup.com

DEDICATION

May this book benefit all those who trust, are trustworthy, have a Trust, and have Trust issues. May the legacy of good Trust planning outlive us all.

ACKNOWLEDGEMENTS

This work was made possible by the genuine and profound support of David Phillips (Estate Planning Made EZ), David Eifrig (Market Wise, Inc. & Stansberry Research), Mark Skousen (FreedomFest), Melodie Gatz (Legacy Global Charities), all the teams at Durfee Law Group, PLLC, the Estate Planning Law Group, Harmony Durfee, Sarah Weldon, Aspen Cashin, Michael Koberlein, Sam Kelsall, and John Goodson. I am also grateful for the incredible clients, advisors, and others who have helped shape this book by sharing their insights and experiences. Of course, no contribution was greater, and nothing matters more to me than my wife, children, and grandchildren. They are my true legacy.

DISCLAIMER

Although the stories and characters in this book are based on actual events and experiences, they are nevertheless entirely fictional. All names, circumstances, and details have been changed to protect the privacy and confidentiality of any actual persons. Any resemblance to actual persons is entirely coincidental and accidental.

The content of this book is necessarily general in nature and is meant to be used for illustration and educational purposes only. This book may not be relied upon as legal advice. The reader is advised to consult with qualified legal counsel and other professional advisors.

DurfeeLawGroup.com/trust-issues-bonus

Visit Durfee Law Group website
for free resources and bonus.

TABLE OF CONTENTS

PREFACE

I built a piece of artistic furniture some time ago. It stayed unfinished in my garage for many years. I tinkered with it off and on, fixing or improving various details. I could never bring myself to put it to use because I was woefully aware of its many imperfections.

One day, a friend saw my creation and asked why I kept it hidden away. When I pointed out the perceived flaws that troubled me, my friend said, "Perfect is the enemy of good." No doubt, he was quoting someone, but neither one of us knew the source of the phrase. I swallowed my pride and put the furniture to use. No one but me has ever noticed its defects.

This book has been much the same. I have worked on it for too long, endlessly tinkering with the inadequacies that irk me. Another good friend has persistently asked me to stop fretting over it and just get it out there. So here it is, flaws and all. This is a work born of long experience. I hope that it does some good for those who read it.

INTRODUCTION

My mother, who loved to bake, often told me that cake and bread have essentially the same ingredients but far different outcomes. You get different results not by changing what you put in, but by the order in which you assemble the ingredients, what you do to them as they are added, and how you handle the raw material once it is assembled.

That same principle applies to what will happen with your wealth over time. There are many competing ideas as to what should happen with your money. The politicians want your wealth, and they have plans for it that do not include providing for your family. Family members may also want your wealth so that they can avoid the trouble of having to work to create their own financial security. Predatory plaintiffs, attorneys, and opportunistic litigants may also want your wealth as a quick means of getting rich.

Families don't have to surrender their dreams for their family or their wealth to power-hungry bureaucrats, relatives suffering from unearned entitlement, or the designs of plundering social pirates. You can build your own independent, long-lasting family and financial structure that is protected from the various circling predators.

Building such a structure that self-perpetuates and outlives you is not a function of how much money you currently have or the situations your family is now experiencing. The structure you build, or don't build, will determine whether your wealth grows or shrinks over time regardless of your starting point. Before you can determine what you should build, you must learn what you can build and the pros and cons of your choices, so that you can recognize what is best to build.

A Trust is one of the central tools of any such plan, one that connects all the other pieces, including the people and the various business and wealth structures. How we put the ingredients of a Trust together and what we do with that Trust over time, completely changes the outcome. If we want a healthy and beneficial result, we must pay attention to the consequences of how the pieces function together.

Centering our focus on trust and Trusts is where we begin to work towards a different outcome than what typical estate planning produces. This book illustrates some of the ways that many commonly used Trusts fail to deliver what people expect from them. It also demonstrates that by changing what we include in a Trust as it is assembled, what we do as assets enter and leave the Trust, and how we handle assets while they are inside the Trust, we can dramatically change the end result.

The purpose of this book is to help remedy the underutilization and misuse of Trusts. For readers who already have a Trust or who plan to create one, this book will help you get the most out of it. It will give you insights that will help you optimize the structure of your Trust and deploy it to the maximum advantage. The principles and ideas in this book will also help you avoid some of the worst pitfalls associated with poorly designed or improperly used Trusts.

You will get more out of this book and out of your Trust if you have your Trust documents readily available to go through as you read. Go get the binder with your Trust in it right now so you can refer to it. Throughout this book, I pose many questions and issues that you will want to address. Writing down your thoughts and impressions as they occur will significantly increase the value of this book to you. I strongly suggest you have a study notebook as you read to collect your ideas.

This book unfolds in three acts:

1. **Understanding the problem** (Chapters 1-3): What a Trust really is, why conventional planning so often fails, and the generational cycle it fuels.
2. **Building the solution** (Chapters 4-7): The foundations of self-governing Trusts, proven principles, integrated systems, and the critical Protector safeguard.
3. **Living the legacy** (Chapters 8-10): Infusing meaning, capturing social capital, preparing future generations, and seeing what success looks like when it all works."

So, now that you're ready, do you trust your Trust?

If you're serious about protecting your family (not just your assets) from the predictable cycle of wealth destruction, then don't stop here.

This book is not about theory; it's a battle-tested roadmap from someone who has seen conventional Trusts fail families time and again, and who has helped build dynasty plans that succeed across generations. The difference between the two paths is not luck or money; it's deliberate design, the right tools, and the courage to think beyond probate and taxes.

Take the next step today:

- Pull out your current Trust (or the folder where it should be) and begin reviewing it with fresh eyes using the questions in Chapter 1.
- Schedule a no-obligation conversation with a qualified advisor who understands multi-generational dynasty planning, not just estate documents. (If you don't yet have one, the resources in this book and at DurfeeLawGroup.com or epmez.com can help you identify the right fit.)

- Initiate a simple family council meeting, even if it's just you and your spouse at first, to discuss what you truly want your legacy to mean.

The choices you make now will echo for decades, possibly centuries. Your family deserves more than a Trust that merely survives your lifetime; they deserve one that helps them thrive long after you're gone.

The question is no longer whether you need a better plan. The question is whether you're ready to build it.

Turn the page. The tools to build a better future for generations to come are waiting.

As we begin with the foundations of Trusts in the next chapter, understanding their true nature is the first step to avoiding the common pitfalls ahead.

CHAPTER 1

IN TRUSTS WE TRUST

TRUST AND THE TRUST

In a troubled world, trust is both rare and precious. Few things merit trust, and those that do are priceless. When trust is lost, it is devastating. Trust is a deliberate action we choose to take. We can also possess or have trust. We can place trust in something. Trust defines a relationship of confidence. For example, people may or may not trust each other. By common usage, a "Trust" is a name for a particular object or thing. Although it did not start that way, at least in the U.S., a Trust has evolved into an entity (which is like a person under the law with its own separate existence).

Trusts are now commonplace. They are used for a multitude of purposes and have become a commodity. Thousands of lawyers, banks, paralegals, financial planners, and online companies make a living selling and administering Trusts. Trusts are the engines that drive estate planning in the United States and many other countries. Almost everyone who has engaged in any level of estate planning has created a Trust. The question at hand is whether their Trust is going to produce the results that they really want.

Even though Trusts are among the most frequently used planning tools, they are also one of the most misunderstood legal instruments. When they are not well understood, Trusts may not be well crafted or effectively implemented. Stunningly, studies consistently show that although they need one, most Americans do not have a Trust or other estate planning in place. We shall also see that there are many people who think they have a Trust when, in fact, they do not.

So, the question is, are Trusts worth the trouble and expense of setting them up? That's what Bob and Sue wondered.

TRASH OR TREASURE?

In a remote and desolate place, a group of shepherds sought shelter from a raging desert storm. The wind blew and sandblasted their faces like scorching hot needles. They found a cave that shielded them from the howling winds. The cave was dark, cold, and filled with trash. They thought the trash, bits and pieces of old paper, was a blessing. It provided fuel for a nice, warm fire. Sometime later, another shepherd, who must have heard of the shelter, found the same cave and what was left of the same trash. The boy wondered if there might be more piles of rubbish than there appeared. He took a piece home and shared it with his family.

As it turned out, the "paper" was parchment, and the so-called trash fit for nothing more than burning on a cold night was, in fact, one of the greatest treasures of all time, the Dead Sea Scrolls.

Like the unrecognized treasures in the cave, Trusts are too often poorly understood, underutilized, poorly drawn, incorrectly implemented, used once and then tossed away, and otherwise burned and wasted. Tremendous benefits and value are lost, and no one is the wiser for it.

HOPES AND WISHES

Bob and Sue had both encountered Trusts without fully recognizing the value of what they discovered.

Bob knew that his great-grandparents had been quite wealthy and that they had a Trust. Once when he asked about it, his parents both glanced at each other and said it was nothing. Just by paying attention to dinner table conversations, he knew the Trust had something to do with why he never saw his aunts and uncles on his father's side.

Sue had been the Successor Trustee of her parents' Trust when they passed. The whole experience made her question the benefit of a Trust. She knew it was supposed to avoid probate, and it was confusing that probate was still necessary with her parents' estate. Even with this experience, Sue was not sure what a probate was, why it was required, and how a Trust could possibly prevent it. She was also frustrated because her parents' Trust had a long title that included both their full names and the words "Revocable Living Trust" and yet she was told it was "irrevocable." The whole thing was a mess, and very confusing.

Bob and Sue's experiences gave them a vague sense that they probably needed a Trust. But they couldn't say why and they weren't completely confident that the need was real. They were not sure of the difference between a Trust and a Will. They wondered if a Living Trust and a Living Will might be the same thing. They went to free dinners about estate planning and heard terms like "revocable" and "irrevocable," but that only added to their confusion. They didn't want to get locked into something they couldn't get out of. It seemed like in the same breath they would be told that a Trust both would and would not protect their assets. It was discouraging.

They knew they wanted to protect their wealth, avoid probate, and not incur estate taxes. They knew that they wanted to make the administration of their estate simple and inexpensive. They loved their children and wanted to provide for them. They wanted their children's lives to be better than their own, and thought that leaving their wealth to them would make that happen. At the same time, they could see that the potential for substance abuse, self-destructive behavior, poor judgement, or divorce could quickly deplete, divert or destroy their wealth. Perhaps more than anything, they wanted to avoid triggering conflict among their children. Having seen the damage that could come from family fights over an inheritance, avoiding litigation was near the top of their list of wishes.

In their heart of hearts, Bob and Sue were more concerned about their family than their money. They had no idea how the two were connected, or what role a Trust might play in that relationship.

For a long time, Bob and Sue did no estate planning because of their many unanswered questions and unresolved concerns. Finally, they relented to the persistent advice of their accountant and investment advisor and decided to go forward with implementing a Trust in spite of their misgivings.

When they asked what a Trust is, they were told it avoids probate, which is good. Bob and Sue's advisors made them feel more comfortable with what they did not know, but did not really close the information gap or address what was really in their hearts. There was little or no discussion about what would happen after avoiding probate, other than that their children would get the money. When they raised concerns about the potential impact on their family, the solution was to make their children wait until they were "old enough" to handle the money.

Sadly, such experiences are not the exception; they are the norm. As common as they are, people who have or inherit a Trust often don't know what they're dealing with. Even those who set up or administer Trusts for a living can have significant misperceptions or gaps in their understanding. The results can be expensive, and lead to poor decisions with unintended consequences.

As we will discover, for Bob and Sue, what they did not know led to disaster. Bob and Sue did not know what they did not know.

DEFINING A TRUST

Trust-like structures have a long history, and can be traced back to a number of ancient legal systems. Modern Trust law in the West evolved in England and is based on common law. The U.S. adopted

English common law in the colonies (with one exception: Louisiana, which bases its laws on the Napoleonic Code). As a result, today, the laws that govern Trusts in the U.S. are primarily derived from common law and, to some extent, have been codified by various state statutes or Trust Codes.

There are many different types of Trusts. Trusts are commonly used in estate planning, asset protection, financial planning, and elder care. In that context, when used correctly, a Trust can: Avoid probate, split property up over time or among different parties, minimize transfer taxes, own and run businesses, and govern what will happen to the property upon specified conditions, such as when a party defaults on a deal, dies or becomes incapacitated. They are also powerful tools for structuring charitable gifts, subdividing real estate, and securing lender interests to finance loans. Trusts may be express (made in writing), or implied (arising from the nature of the parties' relationship), or remedial (imposed as an equitable remedy by a court).

Meaningful answers to the question of what a Trust is can be obscured by talking about what Trusts may do, or the results that a Trust can produce, or how a Trust comes into existence.

While functional descriptions of what Trusts do or accomplish are helpful, they beg the question: What is a Trust?

A PRIVATE CONTRACT

In its simplest terms, a Trust is an arrangement that governs property over time. Unless imposed by a court, this arrangement is contractual and entered into by agreement. As a contract, there are a minimum of three parties to a Trust, and sometimes more: 1) a Grantor who creates the Trust, 2) a Trustee who administers the Trust, and 3) a Beneficiary who enjoys the property held by the Trust. A Trust must also own assets or property. In general, a Trust arises when a Grantor transfers property to a Trustee in Trust for the benefit of a Beneficiary.

Because a Trust has at least three parties, it can be symbolized with a triangle.

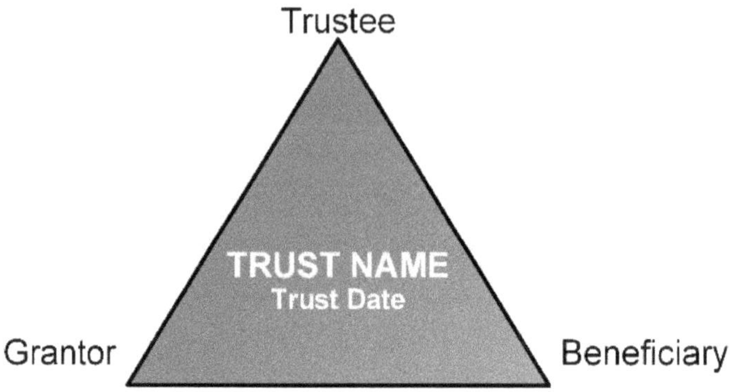

Let's explore in more detail what these terms mean. The instrument or document creating a Trust will employ specific terms or words for each party. Knowing what the words mean helps the parties understand who does what and how the Trust operates. When the parties to a Trust are not on the same page (both literally in the Trust document and figuratively with their respective expectations), it often means one or more of them do not understand their role. Let's start with the essentials.

The "Grantor" is the party who creates the Trust. This party generally gets to make the rules and may or may not have the power to change the rules. There are other words for Grantor, such as Trustor, Settlor, Trust Maker, or Trust Creator. For purposes in this book and in general, I use the term "Grantor" over the alternatives for several reasons. The term "Grantor" is used frequently in the tax code, making the tax relationship between the Trust and the party creating the Trust more apparent. For example, a "Grantor Trust" is a Trust where all the income tax consequences are picked up on the tax returns of the Grantor. Most revocable Trusts are Grantor Trusts.

The "Trustee" is the party who serves as the executive or officer that runs, administers, or operates the Trust. The Trustees must follow the Grantor's intent as spelled out in the Trust document. This Trust arrangement creates what is sometimes called a "fiduciary relationship." The Trustee is a fiduciary with both the legal authority and the duty or obligation to carry out the provisions of the Trust. The Grantor is typically the initial Trustee of most revocable Trusts. With a few significant exceptions, the Grantor will generally not be the Trustee of an Irrevocable Trust. The Trust document will define a lineup of or a mechanism for appointing "Successor Trustees" who become Trustees as prior Trustees pass away, are incapacitated, or resign.

The "Beneficiary" is the party or parties who receive benefits from the Trust. A Beneficiary may or may not get to decide what happens with the Trust, depending on what rules the Grantor establishes. With most revocable Trusts, the Grantor will also be the initial Beneficiary. When the Grantor is also the Trustee and the Beneficiary, it is sometimes called a "self-settled Trust." Such arrangements have consequences for both tax and asset protection purposes. A Beneficiary can be a person or an entity such as a charitable organization. The Trust document will generally define who will become a Beneficiary over time as prior Beneficiaries pass away.

Who serves or should serve as Grantor, Trustee, and/or Beneficiary depends in part on the purpose and terms of the Trust. For Trusts established to protect assets or avoid transfer taxes, the Grantor, Trustee, and Beneficiary typically will not or cannot be the same person.

CREATING A TRUST

Most Trusts have a governing document, contract, or Trust Agreement. A Trust created by a document is technically referred to as an express Trust. Such documentation may take the form of a declaration of Trust, a Trust deed, a Trust settlement, a Trust agreement, or a variety of other contractual forms. The various forms for the document establishing the Trust explain why there are alternative words for the role of Grantor.

No matter what is written on the governing paper, a Trust does not come into existence until a Grantor transfers assets to a Trustee for a Beneficiary. A Trust must own property or assets. No assets, no Trust. This means a Trust is formed when a Grantor gives property to a Trustee to benefit a Beneficiary. This means a person may purchase a pretty binder with a lovely document called a "Trust," which is, in fact, not actually a Trust unless or until someone transfers assets to the Trustee under the terms of the Trust instrument.

Transferring assets to a Trust (or to the Trustee under the terms of the Trust) is called "funding" a Trust. As we will see, a Trust can fail or fall short of meeting expectations when it is not properly funded.

TRUST ASSETS

When you create a Trust, your Trust will be "funded" when you, as the Grantor, convey assets to it. Which assets you convey to the Trust depends in part on what kind of Trust you are setting up. For a typical "revocable" Trust, this will often include appropriate legal documentation such as assignments, deeds, or beneficiary designations that legally convey title or ownership of assets to the Trust, such as:

- Personal property, household goods, and employment benefits
- Digital assets
- Real Estate
- Bank and financial accounts
- Business entities (LLCs, corporations, limited partnerships)
- Intellectual Property
- All other assets of any kind or nature belonging to the Grantor

Some assets cannot or should not be put in a Trust while you are living. As a result, with a revocable Trust, it is typical to make the Trust a Pay On Death (POD) or Transfer On Death (TOD) beneficiary of certain assets such as:

- IRAs and other retirement accounts (after a spousal beneficiary)
- Annuities
- Life Insurance
- Certain business entities

Irrevocable Trusts, Charitable Trusts, and other special purpose Trusts will generally own different assets and have their own funding mechanisms.

In addition to accurately describing the asset going into the Trust, ownership documents that fund a Trust typically need to include at least three pieces of identifying information: the Trustee, the Trust name, and the Trust date. Although some people and institutions believe this information's order matters, it does not. It can appear in any order. A common way for the ownership information to appear is:

The ABC Trust, dated January 1, 2025
Bob and Sue Lastname, Trustees

Every state recognizes either by statute or by common law that this and other essential Trust information can be spelled out in a "Certificate of Trust" which is an abbreviated and redacted form of a longer Trust Agreement. A Certificate of Trust may be updated from time to time as the Trustee and other information change. Most of the time, providing the Certificate of Trust alone to a financial institution or title company is sufficient, and the entire Trust document is not required. Some states even impose penalties if institutions demand more than a Certificate of Trust.

To exist, the Trust must have all three parties and own assets: a Grantor, a Trustee, Beneficiaries, and assets. If any one of these is missing or deficient, the Trust does not come into existence.

REVOCABLE VS. IRREVOCABLE TRUSTS

In general, a typical "revocable" Trust can be revoked, amended or changed by the Grantor. With rare exceptions, the assets in a revocable Trust will be available to the creditors and liabilities of the Grantors, and will also be included in the taxable estate of Grantors. A revocable Trust will be part of an asset protection plan, but on its own does not provide asset protection.

In general, a typical "irrevocable" Trust cannot be revoked, amended or changed by the Grantor. When appropriately structured and funded, the assets in an irrevocable Trust will not be included in the taxable estate of the Grantor, and will be protected from the creditors and liabilities of the Grantor. Importantly, an irrevocable "dynasty" Trust will also be excluded from the taxable estates of subsequent generations, as well as insulated from their creditors.

Such generalizations have a number of exceptions and qualifications. Sophisticated and advanced estate, business and tax plans will often include both revocable and irrevocable Trusts in combination with business entities structured between or among them.

TRUST RULES

The rules that govern the Trust and the relationships of all these parties depend on the Grantor's written intent. This is generally determined by what the Trust document says. The quality and completeness of the language in the Trust document are the root of most Trust issues. When the rules are vague, ambiguous, incomplete, self-defeating, or otherwise ineffective, the benefits of a Trust are lost or diluted.

Notably, and perhaps most importantly, creating a Trust does NOT require a state or government filing, license, or permission. Business entities such as corporations or limited liability companies arise under state charter when applicable paperwork is filed or registered with a governmental authority. Trusts are different. They arise privately, by contract, as property owners exercise their inherent rights to deal with their property as they see fit. Trusts operate within the protection provided by the state and subject to the laws of the state, but do not derive their power or capacity to act from the state.

Failing to understand and intentionally apply the contractual nature of establishing a Trust to fulfill all of its capability and purposes is the cause of most Trust mischief.

Recognizing what a Trust is or can be makes it possible to unlock and gain the tremendous value that Trusts can provide. We can do more with Trusts when we see them for what they really are. Once we know what a Trust is and the vast scope of what a Trust has the potential to accomplish, we can explore what a Trust should do to address and resolve the deep underlying concerns like those of Bob and Sue.

A Trust is an arrangement that governs property over time. Unless imposed by a court, this arrangement is contractual and entered into by agreement.

DOES IT MATTER?

If you are thinking about implementing a Trust but don't have one yet, consider the following:

- What core value do you want your Trust to embody for future generations?
- What small action can you take today to start exploring Trust options that align with your legacy vision?

If you have a Trust, look through it and determine the following:

- Who are your Successor Trustees?
- Have you done all that it takes to actually establish a Trust?
- Is your Trust funded?
- Is there a schedule that lists assets owned by your Trust?
- Did you execute and record a deed conveying your home to your Trust, and can you find a copy or PDF of that document?
- Are your personal bank accounts titled in the name of your Trust or alternatively is your Trust listed as the P.O.D. beneficiary?
- After your spouse, is your Trust the named beneficiary of your retirement accounts, annuities and life insurance?
- If you have a business entity, is it owned by your Trust?
- How hard was it to find this information? Was it displayed in the beginning of the Trust document or on schedules, or was the information buried deep in the document?
- Based on what you've just reviewed, write down the single most urgent gap you found in your Trust and who you'll call this week to address it.

CHAPTER 2

TRUST TROUBLE – THE COST OF CONVENTIONAL PLANNING

HOPES, MISGIVINGS, AND FALSE SECURITY

Once they decided to move forward with a Trust, Bob and Sue asked around and found a local well-respected attorney who practiced estate planning.

They asked the attorney what they should do. The attorney presented them with an order form that listed several options. The attorney talked through each alternative, what was included, and what it cost. "Which package is best for us?" Bob and Sue asked. The attorney told them they needed a Trust.

Bob and Sue felt like their questions were either answered or that they must not matter. Avoiding probate sounded good. The attorney seemed knowledgeable and used many legal words that they did not entirely understand. However, they had confidence in the attorney's good reputation and professional expertise, so they went ahead with the recommended package.

Bob and Sue were not sure of what it meant, but they had a Trust. Their minds were at ease, and they thought they were done. They believed they had some sort of asset protection, that they would completely avoid legal action with their family and estate, that there would be no taxes on their assets at their passing, that their children and grandchildren would be set for life, and that their planning was complete and finished.

They were wrong. What did they have?

THE FALL OF BOB AND SUE

Bob and Sue paid what seemed like a significant amount for the advice and protection. They had every reason to believe their Trust was a good one. In fact, it was well-crafted and comprehensive. Unfortunately, they didn't really know what they had, and the design of the Trust and how they utilized it were fundamentally inadequate for unexpected events.

Because they had a Trust, the happy couple thought and acted as if they had asset protection. Then there was a lawsuit. While they didn't lose everything, they lost far more than they could afford. They thought the Trust would protect their assets, but it didn't. Although they had liability insurance, it was not enough. The legal fees were almost as bad as the damages they had to pay. The ordeal was a disaster not only for Bob and Sue personally but also for the future they had hoped to secure for their children and grandchildren.

Bob and Sue still tried to help their children financially, but to a lesser degree than they had imagined. Partly out of guilt for all the money they had lost and the time spent fighting the lawsuit and working instead of being with their children, they lavished and indulged their children to excess. The more they gave their children, the more their children seemed to need.

In his final years, Bob's declining health and mental acuity led to the need for an expensive and intrusive conservatorship and guardianship. The Trust failed to prevent the need for judicial intervention in their private lives. They had to pay for multiple attorneys, including one appointed by the court, to look into their finances. Bob was compelled to undergo a medical examination to assess his competence. Every year for the rest of Bob's life, they had to report to the court and pay accounting and legal fees.

The intrusive examinations and legal micromanagement were deeply humiliating for Bob. Although incapacitated, he still had enough awareness to understand that he had lost control. Frustrated by the indignity and the hassles they had to endure. Sue found her caregiving efforts increasingly burdensome. Both felt powerless as their wealth stagnated under the administrative burden. Living under the supervision of the court was far from the bright future they had envisioned when they had planned their retirement.

While Bob and Sue endured these personal humiliations and financial drains during their lifetimes, the true long-term damage of their inadequate Trust became evident only after their passing when Generation Two inherited what remained.

GENERATION TWO TAKES CHARGE

Despite the huge losses and disappointments, Bob and Sue still left a substantial amount of wealth to their heirs, partly due to life insurance policies, retirement accounts, business enterprises, and illiquid properties. Ironically, this just added fuel to the fire. Bob and Sue's children didn't light the fire, but they certainly felt the heat.

After Bob and Sue passed away, their estate was tied up in court for over a year. Contrary to their expectations, simply having a Trust was not enough to prevent probate. Bob and Sue had neglected to fund their Trust. They had not transferred any of their assets into it. Their lawyer told them to do so, and some of their bank accounts were in the Trust. But none of the real estate or businesses were in the Trust. The lawyer who set up their Trust indicated that such assets required a real estate attorney or a business attorney, not an estate planner.

Because the Trust was never properly funded and lacked safeguards against family discord, the very mechanism intended to preserve harmony instead became the catalyst for open conflict among the children. In short, their estate plan backfired and triggered dissent and delay due to the process required to fund their Trust after they had passed. The open court proceedings in probate seemed to invite and even encourage conflict. The Trust utterly failed to prevent legal contests among the children, leading to skyrocketing litigation costs and fees. The ensuing family battleground became a lawyer's feeding frenzy. Even family members who didn't want to fight had to engage legal counsel just to protect themselves from predatory siblings.

The children of generation two disagreed with each other and with Bob and Sue's decisions. Each felt that they alone were entitled to be in charge and did not trust any other family member with the task of administering the estate. Through the courts, significant portions of the Trust Bob and Sue had established were either thrown out or changed. The protections that Bob and Sue believed were built into the Trust ended up being completely ignored because the Trust distributed the assets to the children outright upon reaching a certain age.

In the children's eyes, the legal fees were a small price to pay to get a bigger share of the money right away and without any restrictions. They sold valuable properties at a discount to raise ready and spendable cash. It was as if Bob and Sue's children were acting out the archetype of battling and corrupt giants from a Greek tragedy. Their greed provoked overreaching, which ultimately destroyed the very assets they coveted.

While the children fought with each other in court, federal estate taxes depleted a major share of the estate. The state where Bob and Sue lived also took a substantial portion of local inheritance taxes. On top of that, there were significant state and federal income taxes, especially on retirement accounts and annuities. Even the life insurance benefits were taxed, something Bob and Sue had no idea was even possible. They certainly did not know that such taxes were a result of having their life insurance owned by the wrong kind of

Trust. They would have been horrified had they known that they were paying life insurance premiums for the benefit of the IRS.

The avaricious kids fought over a smaller and continually shrinking piece of the pie. Resources that Bob and Sue intended for their children ended up going to lawyers and politicians. In the end, Bob and Sue's estate was divided, disbursed, diluted, dismantled, dumped out of the Trust, and ultimately destroyed. Although their net estate ultimately turned out to be much smaller than Bob and Sue had believed it would be, it was still enough to tear the family apart, break familial bonds, and facilitate personal and familial destruction.

It is a universal and natural law that unearned wealth is not respected. There is no virtue in spending money someone else earned. The children quickly dispatched what was left of the wealth. The Trust that Bob and Sue had counted on to help their family lacked any provisions to curb consumption. With unearned money in hand, the children saw no need to work or grow their inherited wealth.

The siblings rarely spoke to each other but enjoyed all the luxuries their unearned inheritance could buy. They spent wildly on expensive toys, travel, play, alcohol, drugs, gambling, and conspicuous consumption. They did not invest in anything, not even their relationships. There was no effort to build equity or value in the family. Casual sex with an increasing variety of partners became the dominant culture. Relationships were single-use, disposable commodities that could be purchased as desired. Most of those who bothered to get married eventually got divorced. The Trust did nothing to prevent the ex-spouses from taking yet another share of Bob and Sue's dwindling estate.

As the wealth declined, the debt increased. The next generation bought on credit what they could not purchase with their parents' money. While they easily let go of the wealth for immediate pleasures, they clung desperately to the appearance of possessing it in abundance. They ran right up to the edge of a fiscal cliff, then leaned precariously over it as far as they could. The Trust provided no guardrails.

Do you think Bob and Sue had any idea that what they did would lead to this outcome? Do you think they had any concept that the nature of the Trust they set up would eventually destroy their family? Of course not. Bob and Sue had the same hopes and dreams for their children that all parents do. They implemented the same kind of estate planning used by everyone they knew. They didn't know there was any other way. Unfortunately, the unintended consequences of what they did not know were devastating. The way they set up and used (or rather misused) their Trust inadvertently created an environment that ruined all their financial plans and dreams. Worse yet, it did no favors to their family members. The very Trust that was meant to protect the family became the instrument of its undoing.

The destruction did not stop with the second generation. The attitudes and habits they modeled were passed down like an inheritance of their own, shaping the expectations and behaviors of Generation Three fueled by unrestricted and unearned wealth.

GENERATION THREE: THE ILLUSION SHATTERS

The children of generation two always acted and appeared as if they were wealthy, which is why Bob and Sue's grandchildren who comprised generation three were annoyed to find out that their wealth had severely declined and was largely illusory. Their parents modeled an attitude of reckless spending and self-indulgence with no thought for the future, so such attitudes dominated the thinking of the family culture.

The grandchildren lived as they were raised. They saw the world through the lens their parents gave them. They both envied and resented their grandparents, who had created the wealth they saw slipping away. They were estranged from and unaware of any sense of what it took to create the declining family wealth. The concept of a unified family had long ago disintegrated. Productive living was a stranger, and plunder was viewed as the only road to riches. Life became about figuring out how to get someone else's money.

The last little dribble of an inheritance that made it to generation three was quickly gone. What wasn't wasted on empty attempts to buy friendship was taken by savvy entrepreneurs whose business models revolve around selling overpriced goods to or buying underpriced assets from third-generation wealth. The grandchildren became a living example of the conventional wisdom that inherited wealth rarely makes it past the third generation.

Ironically, by generation three, Bob and Sue's family was shrinking. What wealth that remained was going to fewer people. This was in part because marriage and having children was viewed as a path to difficulty and disfunction. Family commitments were perceived as an obstacle to enjoying wealth.

Bob and Sue's troubling story is not the exception; it is the rule. Such events repeat themselves to varying degrees over and over again. Estate planning professionals who are paying attention to the long-term consequences of the advice they give their clients see this kind of family drama played out every day. It is a chronic ailment that infects our entire society.

But it doesn't have to be that way. There is a better way that can lead to an entirely different outcome.

THE BIG PICTURE: THIS IS THE RULE, NOT THE EXCEPTION

Bob and Sue's experience is not limited to the wealthy. It happens even in families with relatively modest estates. A once-beautiful but aging lifted pickup truck sometimes passes me on the way to my office. In the back window is a sticker that says "In Loving Memory of [Grandma] and [Grandpa]." I don't know the driver and I didn't know his grandparents. But I once met his sister. She lamented to me that when their grandparents passed, she inherited their home and some cash. They left her brother a modest rental home. He ignored everyone's advice to keep the rental property. Instead, he sold it and used the proceeds to "invest" in a big truck. She told me he is an honorable and hard-working young man, which is a good thing because his inheritance has bald tires, worn-out brakes, and a nasty oil leak. Working hard is the only way he's ever going to continue driving his investment.

A well-crafted Trust could have produced a different outcome.

WHAT ABOUT THE TRUST? TROUBLING QUESTIONS

But what about Bob and Sue's Trust? When we dig deeply, many troubling questions surround the Trust.

If Trusts are so useful, why do so many people who have them still end up with their estates in probate?

Why do so many people with Trusts still end up paying estate taxes?

Why do so many who set up Trusts still lose their assets to litigation?

Virtually every state has courts devoted explicitly to handling cases involving Trusts. Why do so many Trusts end up in the courtroom?

If a Trust can solve so many problems, why do people with Trusts still face the very troubles Trusts are meant to prevent?

Why are so-called "trust fund babies" stereotypically unproductive, spoiled, dependent, indulgent, and wasted?

Given the enormous effort and resources deployed in putting together Trusts for the purpose of passing wealth on to future generations, inheriting a Trust should have a positive connotation instead of a stigma. The Beneficiaries of Trusts ought to be the most effective and useful members of society instead of the least. The Beneficiaries of Trusts should be those who contribute the most and provide the greatest service and innovation, so badly needed in this troubled world, rather than being some of the least productive and most conspicuous consumers. Families with Trusts should be growing and thriving rather than shrinking and struggling.

Since the whole point of a Trust is to prevent problems, if it causes or aggravates problems instead, we are doing something wrong. There must be something going on in the proverbial blind spot behind us that we can't see. When we turn and look to see the aftermath of what typically happens with most Trusts, it will change how we approach the planning process.

Attorneys who work both sides of Trust planning, setting them up for the living and administering them for the deceased, regularly deal with these issues. Some attorneys find business opportunities and a marvelous cash flow machine in the perpetual flow of Trust issues. The more problems the family has with the Trust, the more money the attorney makes. The more honorable attorneys, however, see both value and opportunity in stemming the tide of trouble and actually preventing the problems rather than perpetuating and profiting from them. When we turn our attention to discovering the cause of such issues and work to help prevent them, everyone wins.

In the chapters that follow, I share some of the worst things I have seen attorneys do or not do. This is not a criticism of all attorneys. There are many excellent and highly qualified attorneys in the estate planning arena. At the same time, even with the best intentions and training, smart attorneys doing what has always been done may inadvertently trigger harmful outcomes for future generations. Hopefully, the concepts in this book will help increase the number of attorneys working to eliminate Trust Issues rather than simply exploiting them or being oblivious to them.

If you already have a Trust or are thinking of setting one up, consider the approach used by the professional planner who created it.

THE OPTIMIZED ANSWER: ORDER-TAKER VS. COACH

Some time ago, I attended a conference of "business consultants." As I went around the room meeting people, I asked each of them what they did and how they helped business owners. The answers were consistent and more or less came down to this: "I ask business owners to tell me what they want, and then I help them get it." That all seemed reasonable enough until I met a consultant with a different answer.

In the entire crowd, there was only one person who took a different approach. This consultant said, "Most business owners aren't qualified to tell me what they want because they don't know what they should want. Too often, business owners want things that not only won't fix their problems but will make them worse. I first coach business owners to recognize what they should want. And then I help them get what they actually need for their business to thrive and succeed."

I met over a hundred business consultants at that event, but I only worked with one of them. I later learned that "working on the business instead of in the business" applied to Trusts as much as it did to entrepreneurial enterprises.

In a similar fashion, many estate planners function like the majority of the consultants I met that day: "Tell me what you want to do with your stuff, and I will tell you how to write it up in a Trust." When planners take this approach, they end up being little more than order takers, circumventing the more fundamental question of what their clients should want.

In reality, most consumers do not have enough information or life experience to know what they should want in a Trust. They may have a general sense that they need one, or that they want to avoid probate and estate taxes, or have some level of asset protection. But beyond that, most people are fuzzy on the details and the consequences of their many options. Sadly, sometimes the reason consumers are under-informed regarding Trusts is that they are getting counsel from estate planning advisors who are equally fuzzy on what a Trust should do.

If they ask meaningful questions, planners will quickly discover that most people have seen or had experience with an inheritance causing trouble, and they want to avoid such issues. In fact, in my experience, people tend to be more concerned about what their estate is going to do to their family than any of the tax or probate issues. This is a difficult line of questioning to meaningfully pursue if the planner has no more than the conventional tools that trigger the kind of trouble experienced by Bob and Sue's family.

When we, as planners, fail to uncover and address the many non-tax and non-probate concerns that people have about their estate and their family, it leads to mismanaged expectations. People who have Trusts expect that the Trust will prevent the problems they are most concerned about. The reality is that a Trust will only do what it was designed to do. If it wasn't designed to address the issues that matter most (impact on family), a Trust isn't going to help and may aggravate or ignite trouble.

Likewise, a single Trust alone is not a cure-all panacea that fixes every issue. Any given Trust can do certain things well, but not all things. A single Trust cannot perform every function. A Trust designed for one purpose may not serve another. There are some functions that are not at all suitable for a Trust and that require business entities. If you believe just having a simple revocable living trust is all you need to plan your estate, protect your assets, reduce your taxes, or prevent family problems, your expectations are not going to match reality.

When there is a disconnect between what you expect your Trust to do and what it is, in fact, designed to accomplish, frustration and disappointment are inevitable. As with Bob and Sue, their poorly designed and implemented Trust created the exact opposite results they had intended for their children.

A Trust is most effective and beneficial when it is tailored to perform particular functions that target optimal outcomes for the family, even if family members don't know enough to ask for such features. A Trust and related structures that aim at anything less than optimal outcomes are, per se, poorly suited and inadequate, and have the capacity to do irreparable damage. An ill-suited Trust can ruin not only wealth but also vital family relationships and individuals.

Far too many families experience the tragic cycle of wealth destruction like Bob and Sue, in part because no one helped them understand what they should want in their Trust. Recognizing that poorly designed Trusts feed the wealth destruction cycle and that such an outcome is problematic is the first step to formulating a viable solution.

The very Trust that was meant to protect the family became the instrument of its undoing.

DOES IT MATTER?

Although Bob and Sue thought they were initiating a multi-generational dynasty, their Trust was instrumental in ripping their family apart and destroying the wealth they had worked so hard to build.

When we base our Trust and estate planning decisions on mistaken beliefs or assumptions, reality comes back to bite us.

- Have you personally witnessed (in your family or others) an inheritance that caused conflict, resentment, or financial waste rather than unity and security?
- If a lawsuit, long-term illness, or incapacity struck your family tomorrow, do you believe your current estate plan (Trust or otherwise) would truly protect your assets and keep your loved ones out of court?

- Have you or anyone you know ever had assets go through probate despite having a Trust in place? What do you think caused that outcome?
- If you already have a Trust (or are planning one), did the advisor who helped you create it ask detailed questions about how you want the inheritance to affect your family's relationships, work ethic, and long-term well-being, and not just taxes and probate?
- Looking at your own family dynamics, what specific problems (e.g., mistrust between siblings, overspending tendencies, entitlement, or divorce risk) worry you most about passing wealth to the next generation?
- Do you know whether your major assets (real estate, business interests, retirement accounts, life insurance) are actually titled in or properly funding your Trust right now? If not, what steps would you need to take to correct that?
- When you picture your family 50 or 100 years from now, what do you hope your wealth will have accomplished: strengthened family bonds, fostered independence and productivity, grown over generations, or something else?
- Does your current estate plan support that vision?

Have you ever considered that a Trust could do more than just divide up assets, avoid probate, and reduce taxes, and that it could include provisions to encourage responsibility, protect against divorce or creditors, or even promote family harmony?

- What features would you want if you could design it with those goals in mind?

[These failures highlight the need for a different foundation; one we examine next in the core principles of self-governing Trusts.]

CHAPTER 3

DON'T THROW DUST IN THE WIND – THE GENERATIONAL WEALTH CYCLE

GREAT EXPECTATIONS

Charles Dickens' classic book, Great Expectations, deals with the social and moral perils of seeking wealth to gain social status without also developing a refined and noble character. The story resonates with readers because we encounter the same dilemma in navigating our own family and wealth challenges. Like many others, Bob and Sue thought that building their personal wealth and putting together a Trust would be enough to protect both their family and their wealth from the conspicuous pitfalls.

They expected that if they had a Trust, the many obstacles to ongoing family prosperity would be removed. There would be no litigation concerning their estate. Their wealth would be protected and preserved and would grow from generation to generation. It would make the lives of them and their children and grandchildren better. Their legal counsel appeared to believe the same thing.

By focusing on the short-term issues of probate avoidance and tax efficiency, they thought they had solved all the problems. They failed to recognize that they were part of a larger drama.

THE FALL AND FUTURE OF DYNASTIES

The great dynasties of Rome, Egypt, Babylon, Persia, China, and the United Kingdom are all moldering in the dust. Let that be a warning to those who hope to leave a legacy for their children, grandchildren, and the generations to follow. The founders of such dynasties sought to create something that would long outlive them. Yet their empires eventually crumbled. The reasons for this are complex, but their inability to think beyond their own lifetime set them on a course that ultimately turned their riches, resources, and culture into distant memories.

This historical pattern repeats today with a vengeance. Nearly every culture has a saying akin to "wealth goes from shirtsleeves to shirtsleeves in three generations." Modern demographics corroborate the cultural anecdotes. The statistics are staggering: Only 57 percent of wealth makes it to generation two, and only about 10 percent makes it to generation three. Wealth dwindles along its way through the family tree until it's all gone, or at least until it has changed hands outside the family. This is the outcome that conventional estate planning and Trusts are producing. If we hope to disrupt this destructive wealth cycle and preserve our family line and wealth in the long-term, we must examine our families and our wealth through a different lens and adopt a different approach.

Ironically, although estate planning Trusts are regarded as a solution to the generational decline of wealth, too often, they are the problem. People establish Trusts to fix specific issues and have no idea that they are actually exacerbating those very problems. We will explore why and how this happens and what to do about it. Doing more of what causes a problem will not solve it.

The difference between being rich and being wealthy lies in what happens to the people and the money over time. The rich are able to enjoy their money while they are living, but when they leave it to the next generation, it often has the unintended result of both wiping out the wealth and disrupting the family. In contrast, the wealthy not only have the ability to enjoy their resources during their lifetimes, but they also have multi-generational plans and structures in place to grow and preserve both the people and the wealth over long periods of time. Achieving this takes more than just a Trust. However, the role a Trust plays in the wealth paradigm will often be the deciding factor in determining whether someone is merely rich or truly wealthy.

Is the purpose of your Trust merely to hand off wealth to the next generation without probate and estate taxes, or would you like to give your descendants self-governance tools and resources so that they can independently grow and protect both themselves and the wealth for multiple generations?

Are you just doing estate planning or "dynasty" planning?

THE NUMBERS DON'T LIE

If "success" means just transferring wealth from one generation to the next, estate planning is failing. The numbers make this clear.

In 2018, U.S. households held a total of $98 trillion in wealth, according to the Board of Governors of the Federal Reserve System's Balance Sheet of Households. Of this, early projections were that by 2030, $15 trillion will be transferred to the next generation. By the year 2055, that amount will rise to $68.4 trillion, impacting 45 million U.S. households. This transfer will be three times the amount of wealth that the previous generation received, but it will be passed to half the number of Beneficiaries. When inflation is factored in, the actual amounts will be significantly larger.

Updated studies give us additional insights. A landmark 20-year study by The Williams Group, examining over 3,200 affluent families, reveals that only about 30% of family wealth typically survives to the second generation, with a mere 10% making it to the third, meaning 70% is lost by the heirs and 90% overall by the time it reaches the grandchildren. These findings, rooted in issues like communication breakdowns (60% of failures) and unprepared heirs (25%), have held steady in analyses through 2025 and highlight why conventional Trusts often accelerate rather than prevent this generational depletion.

The most recent studies now indicate that the so-called Great Wealth Transfer is projected to encompass $124 trillion in U.S. assets through 2048 (up from earlier $84 trillion estimates by 2045), marks an unprecedented shift from Baby Boomers and the Silent Generation to Gen X, Millennials, and Gen Z, with annual transfers already reaching $1.5-$2 trillion and Gen X inheriting the most in the near term at $14 trillion over the next decade, followed by Millennials at $45.6 trillion over 25 years. This surge concentrates wealth more intensely than ever, as smaller family sizes, longer lifespans, and the dominance of high-net-worth households (comprising just 2% but contributing over 50% of the total) result in larger per-person inheritances funneling to fewer beneficiaries. The top 10% will receive 56% of transfers while the bottom 50% will get only 8%. This pending wealth transfer heightens the urgency for dynasty estate planning over conventional Trusts, as standard revocable living Trusts are not equipped to mitigate the "shirtsleeves to shirtsleeves" cycle of wealth loss by the third generation.

The traditional approach to mitigating this generational wealth deflation is to spread out distributions based on age. Most conventional Trusts distribute assets in stages: Beneficiaries receive a portion on one birthday and a bit more a few years later, and the full amount by a certain age. The rationale is that they can't blow it all at once, and they will be wiser by the time they're older. However, despite this, the money is nearly always gone by the third generation. The persistent depletion of wealth over so few generations makes it stunningly clear that the typical approach does not work.

A significant part of the problem is not just poor planning, but often no planning at all. According to the U.S. Trust Insights on Wealth and Worth, only 3 percent of parents believe they owe their children an inheritance, and only 75 percent say it is important to leave children a Trust. This attitude leaves many families to navigate the transfer of wealth without any guidance or planning from their parents. The planning vacuum compels families to seek judicial intervention through the probate courts to obtain and divide up the assets.

It is no wonder that conflict and litigation occur in the next generations over inherited wealth at roughly the same rate as divorce in the U.S., just over 50 percent of the time.

THE ESTATE PLANNING GLASS SHATTERS

If your entire estate plan consists of deciding what will happen to your possessions after you die, you have put your wealth and your family's future happiness at risk. You are surrendering the outcome to the destructive wealth cycle. You are doing the same thing everyone else does and will get the same result.

Elon Musk said, "The most common error of a smart engineer is to optimize a thing that should not exist." Smart estate planning attorneys fall into the same trap when they think that optimizing a Trust is all about being increasingly precise, crisp, and unambiguously clear about memorializing their clients' intent on how to divide up their property. Detailing who will get what may be essential in an estate plan, but it is not sufficient if we hope to disrupt the wealth destruction cycle.

A plan that protects and preserves wealth will unavoidably be multi-generational. If the wealth is not destroyed or depleted but grows over time, each generation will build more and leave more to the next generation than they received. This kind of planning is what I refer to in this book as a "Dynasty Plan" or a "Dynasty Trust." For a Dynasty Plan to be effective, it must encompass and address all the variables that matter, not just the temporal material wealth. First and foremost, such a plan is all about the people.

The focus on the stuff we leave behind distracts us from a crucial fact. What is really going to outlive us? Our wealth or people? Wealth is a thing. It does not live. People live. The stuff alone has no value if there are no people to appreciate it. Without people, the stuff has no meaning or significance. Nature does not discriminate based on wealth. Even the rich are mortal and fallible.

Whether we have children or leave our assets to charity (or to the politicians and the lawyers for those who fail to plan), the people matter more than the property. If we preserve the wealth only to have it destroy the people who get it, have we succeeded? Even charitable causes and institutions, like families, can be derailed or hijacked and work in opposition to the philanthropic objectives of their founders. If we don't protect the people, it doesn't matter what we do with the property. To protect wealth, we first protect the people.

Ultimately, the money we leave behind means nothing. Only the people matter. Living well and leaving a legacy that doesn't dissipate within a generation or two requires action, well-planned, highly targeted (not just on the stuff but also on the people), and properly implemented action.

Importantly, a Trust does not exist in isolation. It is deeply connected to the people. A poorly crafted Trust will expose and exacerbate family dysfunction. A well-crafted Trust may not cure such dysfunction, but it can mitigate the damage. Part of getting the best out of any Trust is recognizing what it will do to the family and what it does with the money.

Think about it. We've all seen inherited money go through a family like a tornado. The wealth destruction cyclone is so common, it's almost cliché. Like dust blowing in the wind, a poorly thought-out Trust can wreak havoc on a family.

WHAT YOU WISH FOR VS. WHAT YOU GET

Bob and Sue's story is a classic example of good intentions being sidetracked and even destroyed by a poorly crafted, underfunded, and badly administered Trust. Far too often, people fail to think about (and plan for) the psychological and emotional impact on children growing up in the shadow of great individuals who started with nothing and built a fortune.

Like many people who create fortunes that seem bigger than life, Bob and Sue were iconic parents. They exemplified the American Dream. Such dreams are the aspirations of the archetypal farm boy who comes to the big city, starts an industry or business, and grows it into an empire. They are the hopes and ambitions of the mom who starts her own small business using skills she learned from her mother and grows it into a thriving commercial enterprise.

Such lofty achievements are beautiful and highly desirable. They also happen to be volatile and have the potential to catapult future generations to even greater accomplishments, or completely destroy them. Danger and opportunity come hand in hand. I sometimes call this "the Daddy Warbucks syndrome" or the "Mommy Warbucks syndrome" based on the old comic strip Little Orphan Annie, which enjoyed various movie and musical theater adaptations.

Mommy and Daddy Warbucks' parents, like Bob and Sue, possess a giant work ethic and a grand vision. They have the ability to marshal capital and people, getting them all moving in the same direction. They use these abilities to create tremendous wealth. They are the wealth producers of the world, enriching those around them as they build their businesses. They are often motivated by a deep desire to shelter their children from the economic hardships they themselves had to endure in their youth or childhood.

Naturally, they want to pass their wealth on to the following generations; that is a fundamental part of the plan. Because the Mommy and Daddy Warbucks parents were hurt by the lack of money, they see giving their children money as a way of protecting them. They mistakenly think that in doing so, they are helping their children. Such powerful wealth producers seem to be the ones most likely to simply hand off wealth to the next generation with a simple

Trust without any thought about what this is going to do to them. All too often, they neglect to prepare the next generations for the burdens and risks that come with spending money someone else made.

The next generation grows up in the shadow of these overachievers. Too often, they are denied significant leadership roles or opportunities in the family business. They are frequently told, "Shut up. I've got this. You can't do it as well as I can. Sit back in your chair, and don't interfere with my business." Ironically, the next generation often gets signals like this from parents who envision building their offspring to be self-reliant producers capable of creating their own wealth. The message of "you must start at the bottom and work your way up just like I did" often gets misinterpreted by the next generation as "you're not good enough, so don't even try." Even when not intended, the message can be that "I must do this for you because you are incapable of doing it for yourself."

Ironically, after shielding their children from hardship and denying them leadership opportunities, the Mommy and Daddy Warbucks parents will expect them to know how to handle the wealth they inherit. Time and again, in working with such parents, we have seen them upset that the upcoming generations have little or no ability to grow and handle wealth in an adult and responsible manner.

Such parents miss the link between denying the next generation leadership opportunities and their inability to grow and wisely use wealth. What the children of wealthy parents know how to do best is spend, because that is the fun and enjoyable part of what they have seen their parents model. Sadly, we have seen such parents end up hating, resenting, and not trusting their own children, and yet still doing everything they can to leave them as much wealth as possible.

Such extraordinary Warbucks parents may produce a great deal of family wealth, but when they fail to prepare their children for the inevitable time when the wealth creators are no longer there, disaster ensues. By the time such parents are gone, the children are typically at or near retirement age and past the time when they can easily acquire the skills and mindset to create and manage wealth. They suddenly find themselves in charge, but without the knowledge, experience, or work ethic that built the family fortune. Even if they're sincere, good, honest, hardworking people, the odds are stacked against them.

Such deferred skill acquisition is like the difference between growing up bilingual and trying to learn a second language for the first time at age 65. When learning is delayed until an advanced age, acquiring fluency is daunting, if not impossible. Having no fluency in the language of wealth, the unskilled next generations are left with the enticing and yet humiliating task of merely consuming. Producing can be out of the question when it's something you've only seen and never accomplished personally.

When this happens, the family's wealth planning devolves. Although they may have inherited wealth in their hands, they don't know what to do with it other than spend it. Instead of being the predator accumulating wealth at the top of the food chain, they become the prey at the bottom of the food chain, a tasty target for others to exploit. The goals shift from creating new wealth to sometimes desperate efforts to avoid loss. They start playing not to lose instead of playing to win. The mindset of "I don't want to mess up what Grandpa gave me" is a different psychology and approach to the game than looking to build one's wealth, with or without the inheritance. Chances are, Grandpa or Grandma never even considered how the way in which they put together their wealth and structured their Trust would change how their descendants think and view the world.

Paradoxically, at the same time, unfettered inherited wealth creates a false sense of security, and the next generation often becomes risk-takers. They think, "I may not be able to do what Grandma did, but I can put my money on this one deal, roll the dice, and win big time." Even level-headed and fiscally cautious people can fall prey to this trap, especially later in life. With an inherited windfall, they suddenly find themselves making big decisions, but their training and experience are too thin for them to discern the good choices from the bad. They imagine they'll inevitably succeed just like Grandpa or Grandma, but without the opportunity to learn from mistakes at an early age, they end up making poor decisions on a larger scale and at an age when there is not enough time to recover.

When people spend or gamble with the money that their parents or grandparents earned without participating in the money-making part of the equation, they are misled into thinking that the skills required for economic success are genetic or a matter of good breeding. They think they can just roll the dice and get lucky. They mistakenly think that is how the wealth producers did it.

Such risk-taking behavior is the result of a failure to transfer life and leadership skills to the next generation along with the inherited money. Such skills can only be acquired through actual life experiences and by making mistakes with enough time to recover. When the wealth building skill set terminates at the passing of the founding family members, the next generation has nowhere to turn for wisdom. Especially in families with wealth, genuine leadership is ultimately not just a function of being in charge. Rather, it is a matter of empowering other family members to lead. True family leaders spend most of their energy helping the upcoming generation learn how to run the show themselves rather than doing it for them.

While the dominant patriarch or matriarch is in charge, if they aren't preparing and training their successors to lead in their absence, they aren't really leading. A top-down "do as you're told" command structure does not result in multi-generational wealth production. It results in people who can sit at their desk and stand in line without talking to their neighbor, but who cannot teach a class. Without an effective and intentional leadership succession plan, there is an inevitable leadership vacuum once the wealth founders are gone.

Successive generations can sense such impending leadership gaps, and often have a fight-or-flight response. They recognize the potential danger and react in one of two extreme ways: family members either refuse to take charge and resent those who do, or they feel that they alone are uniquely entitled to be in charge, and bulldoze and bully anyone who gets in their way. Naturally, others in the family share these thoughts, leading to conflict and distrust. Often, those least qualified to lead are the most eager to seize control and fend off others. Winning the fight among potential heirs to the throne is confused with actual leadership.

Given the opportunities they present, there are industries and law firms with business plans based on exploiting such family dysfunction. This is in part a result of the traditional way in which estates have been planned and administered.

Such human tendencies are part of the real world and will impact the outcome of every estate plan. When a Trust is designed and loaded with tools designed to address such issues, it can balance the need to create opportunities for growth, self-governance, leadership opportunities, and access to capital for future generations, with the need for guardrails that can protect both the people and the wealth when life's dramas go sideways. Such a Trust will enhance both the family wealth and the family bonds over time. The alternative is a time bomb that explodes when the wealth producers die.

The Warbucks Parent syndrome runs deep. Approximately 95% of the top 1% of the wealthy are first-generation wealth. Their parents were relatively poor. They made the money themselves. They are the "Warbucks Parents." Their children are the Warbucks' next generation. When distributed outright to the next generation, the half-life of the inherited wealth is roughly eight years. By year twenty or twenty-four, it is mostly gone, which is why only 9% of inherited wealth makes it to generation three. The next generation of Warbucks children are the trust-babies who blow through their parents' accumulated wealth.

Disrupting this cycle requires doing something different. It requires that "something more." Perhaps we can discover something more from those who have escaped the nasty cycle of burning through money and people.

When we are not fooled into thinking that a Trust's only function is to manage the transfer of assets at death, we open up the possibility of creating far greater and more beneficial structures that flow and grow wealth and actually help the family long after the founders are gone.

Such an outcome also depends on having a deeper understanding of what a Trust is or should be in order to avoid other common mistakes that can prevent a family from thriving over multiple generations.

The difference between being rich and being wealthy lies in what happens to the people and the money over time.

DOES IT MATTER?

Pull out a piece of paper and get a writing utensil. On paper, in your own handwriting, make a bullet list of the following:

- What really matters to you more than anything else?
- What would you like to be going on regarding what matters to you most a century from now, when you and everyone who has ever personally known you are gone?
- Did the wealth founders in your family prepare the next generation to produce, or just to receive? What did that look like, and what was the result?
- What is one specific skill or experience you can give the next generation now — while there's still time — that will help them be producers rather than consumers?

- If you have inherited a Trust or are the Beneficiary of an estate because of a loved one's passing, or are just experiencing a sudden increase in wealth (like winning the lottery), this will help you stay grounded and avoid some of the pitfalls: For at least a year don't sell your house, buy a car, or change your lifestyle. It takes a year for your brain to wrap itself around what you're dealing with. Take a retreat. Invest some time to go to a place where you can be alone and where you are not going to be pestered or harassed by hucksters trying to get at your newfound money. Protect your privacy. Put together an advisory team: a good lawyer, a good CPA, and a good financial manager, all of whom should be independent but willing and able to work together as a team. That is a key component of an integrated plan.
- What does the little voice inside your heart whisper that you should do about it?

These failures show why conventional planning so often falls short. Next we explore the foundations of a truly self-governing Trust that can break the cycle.

CHAPTER 4

TRUST GENESIS – FOUNDATIONS OF A SELF-GOVERNING TRUST

THE PRIVATE POWER OF SELF-GOVERNANCE

Fundamentally, because Trusts are contracts between private parties exercising their property rights, they do not require permission from any governmental authority to come into existence or to operate. Trusts must follow the law. But within the framework of lawful property rights, Trusts can be created and operate by their own rules. When appropriately crafted, a Trust has the capacity to do anything with its property that an individual can do.

When those setting up Trusts do not understand or come to terms with this principle of self-governance, they leave big holes and ambiguities in the Trust document that lead to trouble. Those who view themselves and others as fundamentally dependent on government for their care or permission to act are particularly vulnerable to misperceptions of how the real-world works.

A well-crafted Trust will not defer to government proclamations but will fully spell out its own rules. When the Trust document is inadequate because it is silent, ambiguous, or unclear on a particular point, the gap is filled in one of several ways: through a court order, a statute, a non-judicial settlement, a party being given interpretive power, or through the actions of a Trust Protector.

Historically, the inadequacies of Trust documents have been filled by court order. When a Trust does not spell out what to do or who is to do it, the parties can ask a judge to tell them what to do and who is to do it. Of course, obtaining such judicial action requires a lawsuit. The result and purpose of such litigation is a court order that clears up a problem. The downsides of this approach are many, including the fact that different courts are not always consistent, and litigation is both expensive and adversarial.

To codify the process, reduce the court's involvement, and set parameters for what the court is to do, most states have passed statutes or "Trust Codes" that fill in the gaps for poorly or inadequately drafted Trusts. In most states, the Trust Code only applies if the Trust document is silent or ambiguous. This means that if the Trust document handles an issue or defines a process, the Trust document controls, not the Trust Code. The Trust Code helps to reduce inconsistent outcomes among courts. However, the Trust Code does not eliminate the need for or reliance on court action. Rather, it simply spells out what rules the court is to impose when government or judicial intervention is invoked in the administration or interpretation of a Trust because the parties can't or won't solve the problems on their own.

Sadly, and surprisingly, some lawyers argue that one state or another is better for forming a Trust because the laws of a particular state are better at compensating for the inadequacies of a Trust document. As we shall see, it is far better to have a robust Trust instrument that does not need or defer to the rules created by politicians and courts through litigation.

When the parties are willing, inadequacies in a Trust instrument can be rectified through private non-judicial settlement agreements. A Trust is a private contract, and in general, the parties to a private contract may agree among themselves what the contract means or how it is to be implemented. Working together in this manner can save time and money by avoiding court intervention. But it requires all the parties to come to an agreement. If there are unresolved conflicts among the parties, this approach is not likely to work.

Finally, even well-crafted Trusts will encounter unexpected circumstances. One way a well-crafted Trust will anticipate and facilitate change, including filling in gaps for any ambiguity or lack of clarity, is to give a neutral party the power to interpret the Trust or, through the use of a Special Trustee or Trust Protector, which is discussed in more detail later in this book.

FILLING THE GAPS VS. GRANTING PERMISSION

When it comes to Trusts, there is a certain mindset with lawyers that I think is really sad because it shows a lack of critical thinking. Some lawyers and judges believe that if something is not expressly permitted or authorized by statute, you can't do it, whatever "it" is. And if it is authorized by statute, it is morally correct, no matter what "it" is, even if it hurts people and destroys or plunders property. As a result, otherwise lawful conduct may not be permitted because there is no statutory recital concerning it, and otherwise ethically repugnant conduct is perfectly fine if it is recognized by statute.

This twisted view is terribly flawed and leads to tremendous mischief. If something is not prohibited by law, you can do it. And even if something is permitted by law, it can still be morally wrong. Free people require no permission from the government to deal with their own property, and governmental permission or the absence of governmental prohibition is not the equivalent of moral correctness.

Laws regarding Trusts arise through court cases (common law), which are decisions made by judges to resolve disputes, and by legislation (statute), which, in general, are decisions made by politicians to implement social policy and resolve ambiguities resulting from conflicting court rulings. Such laws recognize and articulate certain aspects of the right to create and administer a Trust but do not create such rights. Likewise, such laws do not preclude the power of private persons to decide what they will do with their Trust.

The Uniform Trust Code and other such laws are, in fact, a response to the problems that arise from poorly drafted, ambiguous, and incomplete Trust documents. When the Trust document is complete and well crafted, there is no need to rely on or defer to what the courts and the politicians have decided is best. People can decide for themselves what is best for their property and their family. A Trust can do anything with property that a natural person can do, and does not require a license or permission from the state to act.

It is important to understand that Trusts can do many things that have no specific mention in the Trust statutes or court cases. When we apply a little critical thinking, it is plain to see that many actions, whatever they may be, are not authorized in the statute because they don't need to be. Unless something is prohibited by statute or otherwise unlawful, it can be done and incorporated into a Trust. You don't need statutory permission to breathe, for example. You can just do it. Likewise, you can do anything that's not against the law in a Trust.

Trusts are necessarily created under and governed by law. The protection and benefits that Trusts provide depend on the law. Trusts operate within the law and are not a mechanism for avoiding or getting around the law. At the same time, the law does not and indeed cannot articulate each and everything a Trust can and cannot do. The law provides a framework within which a Trust operates. However, the governing framework does not dictate or micromanage the details and nuances of what happens. A Trust that claims the protection of the law must comply with the law, but it is not required to leave decisions up to the law that can be made privately.

For example, although there are some exceptions in other cultures and legal systems, the law in the U.S. does not mandate how one must allocate one's assets among family members. Nevertheless, in instances where we have not properly documented our intentions, the law provides default presumptive allocations among family members, known as "intestate" rules. Confusion can result from the dissonance between being able to do as we wish with our property and the presumptive rules that apply if our wishes are not known.

Unfortunately, although the default Trust rules that politicians put in the statutes may be beneficial in some instances, they are not always what's best in every instance. The people who make the rules can change the rules. That's what politicians do. As a result, a Trust that depends on statute can be modified or amended without the consent of its constituents. Even without action by the politicians, you or your family or your property may be in a different place in the future than where it is today, and as a result, the laws of that future location may end up controlling your affairs. It is far better for a Trust to deliberately spell out its own rules rather than simply rely on politically derived statutes to make up for incomplete or inadequate language.

Although it takes more work, professional judgment, and thinking through the issues for the attorney, a well-crafted Trust will not simply defer to or depend on statute. A well-built Trust will spell out the rules that are in the best interest of the parties to the Trust. When the governing rules are all contained in the Trust, it will be simple and easy to know where to look for the rules in future years. The Trust will be self-contained and not be subject to the ebb and flow of politics or where the people or the property may happen to be located. The only real downside of spelling out all the rules in the Trust is that it makes the Trust instrument longer and more complicated.

That's where an attorney or law firm experienced in Trusts brings value to the table. This is also where attorneys who are just renting forms and don't understand what the forms do can be dangerous. The client is best served when the lawyer carefully exercises professional judgment about what rules are going to be best for the client within the given set of facts, the family situations, and their assets. What rules are going to get the job done? An experienced attorney will have a library of provisions with many different variations to address different situations.

Which rule is best will depend on many factors, such as marital status, the size of the estate, whether the children are Trustees or not Trustees, whether or not the Trust owns businesses, how well the next generation works together, and the competency level of the next generation to handle the assets and the administration of the estate. It is dangerous and not in the client's best interest to leave the ability of the Trust to accomplish its objectives over the years to the politicians. At the risk of offending some of my peers, let me be clear: Depending upon and deferring to the Trust Code rather than crafting provisions that are in the best interest of the client is a sign of sloppy, lazy, poorly thought-out, and ineffective legal work.

Just because most Trusts have done things in a certain way in the past does not mean we are restricted to doing them the same way going forward. We can use Trusts as tools of innovation in wealth and family preservation. Understanding this and using innovation and inherent property rights to the advantage of the family and parties to a Trust is one of the factors that distinguish low-grade entry-level Trusts from highly functional multi-generational long-term Trusts.

Let's explore some of the things that a well-crafted and highly developed forward-looking Trust will or will not do.

SPELL IT OUT

What goes into the language of a Trust determines whether or not a particular Trust instrument will deliver the outcome you want. This elevates the significance of the skill level and outlook on multigenerational planning of who wrote your Trust.

You have several options for crafting the rules that will govern your Trust. You can write the rules. You can use a Do-It-Yourself form or an online tool. You can use a paralegal or financial services provider to fill out such forms with you or for you. You can work with an attorney who uses fill-in-the-blank forms purchased online. You can work with a law firm that develops and maintains its own templates and forms to build customized documents.

As we shall see, each has its own benefits and hazards.

Bob's brother, Jim, was a smart guy, very smart. He was an engineer by training, "old school" in his approach. He learned engineering when the most sophisticated calculating device was a slide rule. Jim believed he was more intelligent than everyone, especially lawyers. He was probably right. But his superior intellect did not save him from a lack of experience and poor judgment.

Jim cobbled together his own Trust. He gathered provisions and components from various contracts and documents he had encountered over the years. He did so by hand. He literally cut and pasted paper provisions onto pages and then photocopied each page. On the one hand, it was a Frankenstein document with a hodgepodge of font types and sizes and visible lines where he had used rubber cement to paste it all together. On the other hand, it was brilliantly assembled, grammatically correct, and structurally organic and sound. It read like a well-formed essay. It had its own beauty and simplicity. Jim loved it and was very proud of it. But in reality, it was a complete hack job.

At his request, multiple attorneys in the law firm where I worked at the time reviewed the document. We came up with a considerable list of problems and issues, and made specific recommendations on how to make the Trust do what Jim mistakenly believed it was doing. Jim would have none of that. He vigorously disagreed with the lawyers' interpretation of the words he had meticulously chosen. He was oblivious to the possibility that words that meant one thing to him, were in fact terms of art with different meanings defined by statute or case law. The Trust was his creation, and in his mind, no one could improve upon it. He stood his ground. Then he died.

Jim had a sizable estate, well over the estate tax threshold at the time. His plan to avoid estate taxes was simple. He gave most of his estate to charity. He had enriched his children while he was alive, and they "wanted for nothing" (even though they wanted everything). Jim expressly excluded them as Beneficiaries of the Trust. However, he also made them the Successor Trustees. Jim was confident that his children would honor his charitable wishes. Jim was wrong.

The children lawyered up and exploited the numerous flaws in the Trust to circumvent Jim's charitable intent. They wanted the sizable estate for themselves and were willing to pay the taxes and legal fees to get as much of it as possible. Although notice to the charitable Beneficiaries was required both by law and by the terms of the Trust, the children as Trustees just ignored that obligation. Simply put, they took the money and ran. What the children did not know or remember was that Jim had given a copy of his Trust to the charities he named. The charities knew about and had been planning on Jim's generous gift.

Litigation ensued, spanning three states and taking several years. In the end, and a considerable amount in legal fees later, the charities were able to collect what was left of the Trust assets. The children were, of course, angry and bitter. They believed that they were entitled to the Trust assets and that they were wrongfully deprived of their family wealth by "money-grubbing" charities and their lawyers. The fallout continues to ripple through Jim's family to this day. Rather than supporting Jim's charitable wishes, they resent them, and feel victimized by their father's foolish generosity.

Jim was undoubtedly smarter than every attorney he had ever met. But he had no idea how a Trust operates over time, what it requires to be legally compliant, or how to make it airtight against challenges and attacks from those who stand to benefit from defeating it.

Don't be like Jim.

Today, it is no longer necessary to cut and paste paper to self-assemble a Trust and other legal documents the way Jim did. As a result of the computer revolution in estate planning, DIY Trust forms and kits are widely available online. Like the lawyers who rent documents referenced previously, consumers can now obtain computer generated documents. Likewise similar to what happens when lawyers rent their forms, the output is determine both by the quality of the templates, and the skill and knowledge of the person filling out the forms.

Most DIY forms are simple fill-in-the-blank templates. The more basic versions turn out to be essentially identical documents for everyone with different names and details inserted in the blanks. More sophisticated DIY documents may have optional provisions that users can select or that are determined by data input or answers to questions.

Some AI-driven models can assist the user in selecting what to include or not include by making suggestions, but there are limits. Using such templates can be like ordering pizza toppings a la carte. You had better know what you like and need, or you'll end up with something you don't want to eat. No amount of computer guidance can tell you what something tastes like. Likewise, no amount of nudging by computer prompts can tell you of the consequences and meaning of how your Trust is going to play out in the lives of your family.

On the one hand, documents created using such tools will typically be superior to Jim's brilliant but flawed cut-and-paste approach. They tend to be cohesive and include the essential legal elements because they are mostly built from a boilerplate that has been used and tested for centuries. At the same time, if used in isolation, what they will be missing is the fine-tuning and adjustments that require the judgment, discretion, and experience that human intellect is uniquely able to provide. I have encountered such documents, which are beautiful and well-written and would be completely appropriate for someone, just not for the person who ended up with them.

Such DIY document templates only get answers to the questions they ask. They don't get answers to the questions that remain unasked. Knowing what questions should be asked is part of what it takes to get a good match between the document and the user. In the end, as "smart" as computers appear to be, they just reassemble and regurgitate the data that is fed to them or that they are programmed to collect. Large language models and data sets may improve the output and may cast the illusion of intelligent creation. But the output will always be a recitation of reworked historical human statements.

Contrary to the pessimism of mechanical determinists, humans create, invent, and solve new problems they have never encountered before. Computers are awesome and powerful tools that can gather, sort, and collate large amounts of information that greatly aid us in our work. But there are some things that require human judgment and discretion, including such things as whether or not to use nuclear weapons on one's enemies, whether we pull the plug on grandma, and the very personal and intimate decisions of life, including those that go into a well-crafted estate plan.

The a la carte approach may be a great way to build a meal. Data gathering and computer-managed decision trees can help narrow the field, track what we have eaten in the past, and inform us about healthy eating choices going forward. But in the end, we decide what we eat. We decide what we enjoy eating and don't enjoy, what we want and don't want, and we can change our minds.

In the same way, computer-driven data gathering and decision protocols may be useful in producing a good rough draft for legal document development. But in the end, we are the ones who must live with the document and experience its consequences. Our lives, our wealth, and the lives and well-being of our family members are on the line. Our personal judgment is essential.

Our judgment will always be improved when we exercise it in the context of input and counsel from an experienced guide who has been down the trail many times with many travelers. A computer may store pictures and measure distances and technical features of a trail. But a human who has actually walked the trail and helped others walk the trail can give perspective and guidance that no computer can ever provide.

Candidly, one of the ways both template-based documents and short-sighted trail guides make things worse rather than better is when they fail to consider the long-term consequences of short-term decisions. Too frequently, by simply doing things the way they have always been done (which is what templated or DIY documents and AI-generated documents are unavoidably built to do), the problems of the past are perpetuated and made worse. They replicate what has been done in the past. What most traditional Trusts have done in the past is not effective at preserving and growing wealth over time. If we keep doing the same things that destroyed wealth in the past, we are just feeding and perpetuating the wealth-destroying fire.

There are circumstances where DIY template-driven documents may be appropriate. The kind of short, simple Trust that DIY forms produce may work best for very small, simple estates with no family drama, where the only goal is to avoid probate. Larger and more complex multi-generational Trusts are better suited for smaller estates when the goals are to protect the estate from in-laws or substance abuse or creditors. Of course, growing wealth multi-generationally requires a tool designed to accomplish that goal. Even when a short and simple Trust may be sufficient, there are so many ways to do it wrong that a DIY Trust is rarely the best option. It is a good idea to get help.

Using DIY forms is a computerized way to be like Jim, who did not know the limits of his own life experience. This is an example of optimizing a process that probably should not exist. The best DIY Trust will simply not give you the same outcome you get when you enlist the aid of a qualified professional advisor in the Trust creation process.

Who are you going to call to help you with your Trust? What makes any advisor "qualified" to give guidance in setting up or updating a Trust? Of course, some legal qualifications can be earned through training and experience. However, the qualifications that make the biggest difference are a matter of perspective and judgement about what really matters most in the world in general and people's lives in particular. Such things are not taught in law school and aren't on the bar exam.

Like my business consultant friends, there are a great many advisors who take the approach of "tell me what you want, and I'll write it up in a Trust for you." However, it is rare for advisors to have a vision for what a Trust should do beyond what it may do. For example, as we have seen, there is a difference between those who see a Trust as just a device to manage our worldly possessions when we die and those who believe it should have a larger and longer-lasting role. Even among those who have a sense of what a Trust should do, there will be strongly held differences of opinion as to what that is. It is important for you to find a good match between what matters most to you and the vision, values, and approach of your advisor.

Setting up a Trust that meets both your short-term and long-term goals and is well suited for your particular family situation and wealth requires the skills and experience of someone who is personally familiar with the path and will guide you in evaluating the very best options for integrating and connecting each of those pieces of your life, wealth and family puzzle. Find an advisor whose vision for what a Trust should do is consistent with your values and what you want for your family and wealth. Such a shared vision between you and your advisors is essential to getting the right fit with your Trust.

How do you find such an advisor? It is highly unlikely that you will find an advisor whose vision corresponds with yours if your selection process is based solely on price, unless, of course, price alone is the extent of your vision. Certainly, there are businesses and individual advisors who will gladly offer super cheap rates to set up a Trust. The low costs may sound like a bargain. It's more than just a matter of getting what you pay for. The question you should ask is, what else are they selling you?

People and places offering Trusts at a low price sometimes run what has come to be known as a "trust mill." If a Trust promoter is only charging a small fee for a Trust, they are probably making money some other way. They're almost always selling you something else. That something else is usually a financial product, such as an annuity. A low-price Trust can be used as a loss leader that gets you to buy something else. The real product in such a business model is not a Trust, it's you.

When it comes right down to it, the resulting Trust instrument is often created by an advisor using DIY forms and filling in the blanks for you. Many of the Trust documents provided by DIY services and through trust mills are essentially the same: very simple and based on antiquated Trust forms. The Trust document will typically be very short and will include just enough to qualify as a Trust and little more. They will not delve into any advanced or long-term planning issues. They certainly won't raise multi-generational or dynasty planning options. This is not necessarily bad, as long as the Trust you get is the Trust you need.

Also, to be clear, there is nothing inherently wrong with the financial products that sometimes come bundled with a Trust. Often, such financial products are a crucial component of effective estate planning. Appropriate financial vehicles help with important planning issues such as retirement planning, long-term care, funding tax liabilities, and cash flow needs. There are many highly qualified and expert financial professionals who hold themselves out as "estate planners" when, in fact, they are not attorneys, and they don't set up Trusts. They make their living through the sale of financial products that are useful and beneficial in the estate planning process. Their insights and counsel can be extremely beneficial.

Here's the big distinguishing factor. The best and most qualified financial professionals, including certified estate planners, will assist their clients in engaging independent qualified legal counsel to put together a Trust and other estate planning legal documents rather than doing it themselves. The different professional perspectives, financial, accounting, tax, and legal, result in the best estate plans.

I would urge caution when a Trust and financial products come as a package deal from a single source. In my experience, an in-house attorney who is bundled with and works exclusively for a financial products provider is less than independent. They, too, may get paid based on the purchase of financial products, rather than on the value of the Trust. This does not mean that they are bad attorneys or that their advice is wrong. It just means they're not entirely independent, and that can have consequences. A truly independent attorney will work with many financial providers and have a standalone law firm that gets paid on the basis of legal fees, and not on the sale of investment or insurance products.

The best advisors will coordinate and collaborate with each other to work as a team for your benefit. None of them will be captive to the other. None of them will disregard the others. None of them will behave like the proverbial hotshot player who must do it all and hog every shot personally without ever passing the ball. Rather, they will work together. Ideally, estate planning is a team sport. You achieve the best results when each advisor brings their professional qualifications to the table and each focuses on contributing their best to execute the play together.

Having such a high-functioning advisory team is part of what we call "integrated planning."

So far, we've noted that attorneys' values, vision, and philosophy will shape their advice and the thought they put into designing a Trust. We've also seen that genuine independence and the ability to work with other advisors as a team matter. Other key factors to consider in finding an attorney are the depth and breadth of the attorney's experience and the scope of services the law firm can provide.

We are now going to explore the actual authorship of most Trusts, the importance of funding your Trust, and what will happen when it is time to administer your Trust.

WHO REALLY WROTE YOUR TRUST?

Charles Dickens noted that attorneys are word mongers. They are in the business of selling words. The words they craft and have available for their clients to acquire will be a function of not only their legal training and experience, but also their view of what is important and their ability to connect their language with the real world. They unavoidably learn and gather words that have a history. Attorneys don't have to reinvent phrases or rewrite the dictionary to come up with their words. They select from the many available options and decide which words will be best suited for their clients. It is fair, reasonable, and appropriate for you to ask who is actually selecting the words in your Trust.

The estate planning industry faces a peculiar challenge that most consumers are unaware of. Today, very few lawyers own or develop their own Trust documents. Prior to the introduction of computers and the internet, every single Trust had to be typed by hand. Lawyers who wanted to do Trust work could go to any bank with a Trust department and obtain valuable templates for Trusts and related documents. That's where I got my first Trust forms, and it gave me a good place to start.

Such document specimens that the banks handed out were fairly uniform. Lawyers would basically fill-in-the-blanks and type out a Trust agreement. It was quick and easy. There was little variation. Because each document had to be individually typed, short was better than long, so the documents were simple. There were very few word choices to be made. It was effective for the time. The system worked, and the banks would recognize and accept the documents. Such simple fill-in-the-blanks templates are still used today in most DIY and online document generation services.

With the advent of computers, estate planning has changed significantly. Trusts are now automated and built by assembling standardized provisions. Trust documents can be longer and more complex, and do much more. This is good for consumers on several levels. Trusts, once so labor-intensive and costly that only the wealthiest could afford them, are now much less expensive to produce and more accessible.

The challenge is that it requires a high level of legal knowledge and time to build, maintain, design, and correctly assemble all the potential Trust provisions. The process of developing such documents is often viewed as a distraction from the income-generating part of a law practice. The more Trusts a lawyer prepares, the more money the lawyer makes. If the lawyer is spending time designing and updating Trust provisions, there is less time to sell Trusts. It's a catch-22.

As a result, a growing number of attorneys who prepare Trusts do not own or develop their own templates. Instead, they purchase document templates from various third-party vendors. In other words, rather than making word choices based on experience, training, and an understanding of the client's needs, they are outsourcing the word choice function.

There is good news and bad news with this arrangement. The good news is that many lawyers collaborate and share input to create high-quality Trust templates. The final work product can be excellent. In the hands of an experienced attorney, the outcome can be spot on for the client's needs.

The bad news is that too many lawyers simply rely on the expertise of others and have no idea what the final Trust document really is or should be, what it does, or how it works. Ready access to such Trust forms lowers the threshold for lawyers to enter the estate planning market. Attorneys with less experience or training can fill in the blanks and crank out nice-looking Trust packages without fully understanding their contents.

Most of the time, having an attorney fill in the blanks in a Trust template will be better than the DIY approach. But the quality of the attorney's input in the word selection process will depend on the attorney's skill level. When attorneys don't understand what the documents are doing, they struggle to explain what they mean and are hardly in a position to give meaningful guidance to their clients as to which words are best.

It has been my experience that lawyers who outsource the Trust documents often do not know what to do with the Trust when their clients pass. Our firm ends up assisting many families with Trusts created by other attorneys because the lawyer who created the Trust does not offer Trust administration services, and is hard pressed to explain how the Trust operates.

The fill-in-the-blank process can also devolve. I have encountered lawyers who download a few templates (for a fee) and then reuse them repeatedly as a one-size-fits-all product (to avoid another fee).

I have seen Trusts put together using such outsourced Trust forms that were excellent in every respect, perfectly crafted, well-written, and legally on point. Sadly, however, they didn't do what the client wanted or needed. For example, I have reviewed Trusts that were generally well-crafted but had some gross errors, like inadvertently disinheriting a family member contrary to the client's wishes. Trust provisions that work well for one client can be catastrophic for another. Like any tool, Trust form subscription services work well for the client of lawyers who know what they are doing, and terribly for clients of lawyers who don't.

Another significant challenge is that the Trust templates built by the consensus of many advisors will reflect the values, philosophy, and word choice of the collective. They tend to optimize doing what has always been done rather than innovating or examining whether what has always been done actually works. Such templates tend to reflect the past rather than anticipate and prepare for the future. It is precisely such traditional estate planning that is feeding and causing the wealth destruction cycle. Again, if we keep doing the same thing, we will keep getting the same results. If the goal is to break that cycle and preserve and grow wealth multi-generationally, it requires a different approach.

Candidly, on the one hand, firms that develop and maintain their own forms have the capacity to produce highly customized and precise Trust instruments. On the other hand, even in such firms there will generally be new and younger attorneys who do not have a long history with the documents or the process to create them. As a result, such firms must have a rigorous training program and require documents prepared by less experienced attorneys to be reviewed by more experienced attorneys. This way, over time, newer attorneys will acquire the skill and experience needed to understand and create Trusts, and they will live through a history of participating in making crucial word choices. In the same way, lawyers who go to the trouble of learning what the outsourced forms they are using actually do are better equipped to produce high-quality work product.

Lawyers will argue about this, but it is my opinion that although it takes time and effort, attorneys who develop and maintain their own Trust forms are more knowledgeable about what the documents do, what the client's choices are, and how to craft a final work product that meets the client's objectives. It also puts them in a better position to figure out and optimize what actually works in multi-generational wealth planning rather than just mimicking what everyone else is doing.

Perhaps it's no coincidence that there appears to be a correlation between a lawyer's understanding of what a Trust is supposed to do and the lawyer's ability to help the client complete essential tasks, such as funding the Trust.

FUNDING FOLLIES

One of the most common pitfalls in setting up a Trust is failing to "fund" it by transferring assets to it. The risk of falling into that hazardous pit increases significantly with DIY Trusts, Trusts created by non-attorney advisors, Trusts assembled by less experienced or knowledgeable attorneys, and Trusts peddled by double-dipping attorneys.

It appears to be the rule that DIY Trusts simply go unfunded, often resulting in probate. Except perhaps for the financial products, you may purchase from the financial advisors who provide Trusts, the typical trust mill will not help you transfer other assets to your Trust. They will not prepare deeds. They simply ignore business entities and assets they cannot "manage" for a fee.

Sharon and her husband Steve were attentive to life's details and planned their estate. They paid an attorney a small amount of money to create a Trust. They were careful to make sure it was a living Trust and not a testamentary Trust because they wanted to avoid the troubles they experienced with the estate of Sharon's parents, Jeremy and Linda. (We will meet them later.) At the same time, they were price-conscious and wanted to save money. Price mattered. They were trying to be fiscally responsible.

The lawyer gave Sharon and Steve a letter advising them to put all their assets in the Trust, including their real estate and bank accounts. The attorney did not, however, prepare any deeds. The attorney knew about but never even mentioned what to do with their company. Business entities were outside his wheelhouse. The attorney was also not concerned about their retirement accounts and life insurance policies because he knew they had each named the other as beneficiary. He told them that naming a beneficiary was all they needed to do. He said nothing about making the Trust a beneficiary, and even if he had, it would have made no difference.

Like so many others, the couple never followed through with the lawyer's advice. When Sharon and Steve passed on, their children discovered that there was a Trust but were surprised to learn that the assets in the estate were essentially frozen. They couldn't sell the house, and they couldn't access the bank accounts.

Steve had outlived Sharon. The children couldn't collect the life insurance on Steve because Sharon was the beneficiary, and since she had passed, the beneficiary became her estate. Likewise, Sharon was the named beneficiary on Steve's retirement accounts, with the same result.

The children also had trouble with Sharon and Steve's company on several levels because the only owners were deceased and not available to deal with the state, the IRS, or the financial institutions with the business accounts.

Sharon and Steve had failed to put everything they own in the Trust, their money, the deed to their house, their business entity, all their assets. They had beneficiaries on life insurance and retirement accounts, but never named the Trust, and failed to update the beneficiary designations when Sharon passed. True, they had a Trust, but it was an empty vessel.

"We have Mom and Dad's Trust. But the bank, the title company, and the insurance company are all telling us that we need 'Letters Testamentary' to access the assets. What gives?" At first, the children could not decipher what "Letters" meant or why they had to have them. Eventually, after calling a lawyer, they learned that this meant the estate had to go to probate. They learned that they could not deal with any of the assets in the estate until they obtained a court order admitting the Will to probate and appointing an Executor or Personal Representative.

The children were furious. "Why do we have to do a probate when there is a Trust? This is the same thing we saw with Grandma and Grandpa (Jeremy and Linda). What a waste of money it was to go to an attorney. The Trust this guy sold us is completely worthless and did us no good whatsoever."

How one's house is owned changes what happens upon passing. If legal title to the house is in the name of Mom and Dad, not the Trust, the benefit of the Trust is lost. Worse yet, we have seen instances where Mom and Dad lived in "their" house for decades, but title to the house was still in the name of their parents, Jeremy and Linda, Grandma and Grandpa, who had been dead for 40 years. In a worst-case scenario, which we have seen more than once, it becomes necessary to do not just one but multiple probates, one for Grandpa, one for Grandma, one for Mom, and one for Dad, all because they were each in the chain of title for the house.

Multiple probates were just the beginning of the problems the family faced. Each of the multiple probates had its own claimants who wanted a share of the wealth and were willing to pay an attorney to fight for it. Even though it was a relatively small estate, the family had to share what they eventually received with several attorneys.

The sadness of losing a beloved relative can be offset somewhat with the benefit of an inheritance. But the pleasure of inherited property is tainted and turns to anger when expensive and adversarial legal proceedings are required. When people don't properly fund their Trusts, they create all kinds of financial, legal, and emotional nightmares for the people they want to inherit their assets. An old song by the Mills Brothers called You Always Hurt the Ones You Love seems appropriate in situations like this. Sadly, they happen all the time.

Every estate must be administered to some degree. Beneficiaries must collect assets, property must be sold or distributed, and taxes must be paid and accounted for. The cost and disruption required to administer an estate go down dramatically when beneficiary designations are updated and appropriate and the Trust is properly and completely funded.

Even with the best of planning and the highest quality and completely funded Trust, the administration of an estate often requires or goes better with assistance from an attorney. Setting aside other intrinsic factors like the size or complexity of the assets and family dynamics, in our experience the most expensive estates to administer are in order of cost 1) DIY Trusts like Jim's, 2) Trusts created by non-attorneys, and 3) Trusts created by attorneys who do not understand or help fund the Trust and, 4) Trusts created by attorneys who do not offer estate administrative services.

DIY Trusts, by their nature, do not involve an attorney. If an attorney's assistance is needed in the estate administration, the family has to go shopping to find one. Trust mills generally focus on selling Trusts, not administering them, and won't be able to help when it's time to administer the Trust after the Grantors pass. This is especially the case if the trust mill is comprised of financial advisors and not attorneys. Trust mills are not equipped to handle the probate and other legal challenges that result from not helping people fund their Trust.

Candidly, our firm has an entire department devoted to helping people administer Trusts and doing probates for those with DIY Trusts or Trusts sold to them by trust mills. While we are able to help clean up other advisors' messes, I still prefer to advocate for not creating the mess in the first place.

In my experience, the client gets a better result when the lawyers who help design and structure Trusts are also familiar with and have experience handling Trust administration and probate. When advisors are familiar with both the planning and administration aspects of legal issues, they can think both backward and forward through the process and help design Trusts that avoid or minimize most of the problems.

Because of such professional experience, our firm receives a lot of calls from people who discover that the lawyer who set up their Trust is either dead or that the law firm doesn't handle Trusts or estate administration. We end up helping a lot of families when they don't know what to do with their deceased parents' Trust. We also bring in young, smart, hard-working attorneys and train them so that when older attorneys retire, slow down, or are otherwise unavailable, there will be attorneys in the firm who are familiar with the clients and their planning and are available to assist with issues as they arise. This is a key component of our firm's 500-year succession plan.

When shopping for someone to help establish a Trust, a savvy consumer will ask questions about what kind of help will be available for the next generation after those who created the Trust are gone. The law firms best suited to assist future generations are those that have their own multi-generational succession and operational plan to be in business when the time comes, long after the attorneys currently working in the firm are gone.

"Stupid is as stupid does," according to Forrest Gump's mother. Lawyers are as lawyers do. Those who understand the significance and far-reaching scope of the succession planning involved in a Trust will have a succession plan for their practice and will be better qualified to advise their clients.

One of the reasons it is beneficial to work with a law firm that both plans estates and administers them for the next generation is that they will be very familiar with the consequences of your choice in Successor Trustees. A law firm with experience on both ends of the process will be better qualified to guide you through the decision-making process.

Don't be like Jim. His Frankenstein DIY Trust might have worked had he not named disinherited family members as Trustees. Selecting Successor Trustees is necessary. Who you pick will impact what happens to both the family members and the assets in your estate.

TRUSTEE SELECTION

Who the Trustee is can have significant tax consequences. To preserve certain tax attributes and to protect assets held by the Trust, certain transactions require a "non-subordinate Trustee" i.e., a Trustee who is not a spouse, sibling, or child of either the Grantor or the Beneficiary. It is vital to designate Trustees who fulfill rather than defeat the essential functions or purposes of the Trust. Even if an independent Trustee is not required for the day-to-day operations of the Trust, a high-functioning Trust will facilitate invoking such a Trustee's action when needed.

Before selecting a Trustee, each option should be carefully evaluated in line with the wishes of the person or family creating the Trust. Naming the wrong Trustee can cause as much or more damage as having a poorly drafted Trust. As we saw with Jim's estate, having the wrong Trustee can defeat or frustrate the purpose of a Trust. There are many options in naming Successor Trustees, each with its own pros and cons:

- Children
- Extended Family Members (siblings, parents, cousins, in-laws)
- Trusted friends
- Professional advisors: CPA, Attorney, or other professional (most financial advisors are not able to serve as a Trustee for their clients because of licensing restrictions).
- Professional or Private Fiduciaries
- Banks and Financial Institutions
- Affiliated Trust Companies associated to some degree with a financial institution or insurance company.
- Independent Trust Companies

Generally, family member Trustees are easier to work with, cost less, and allow greater flexibility. However, such flexibility can lead to an increased risk of abuse, neglect, or corruption. There are times when it may be far better not to have a family member serve as a Trustee. This is particularly true when there is:

- a risk of family conflict
- a lack of trust or willingness to work together
- a lack of financial sophistication
- a pattern of financial indifference or neglect
- trouble with the law
- addictions or mental health care concerns
- only minor children
- children from more than one marriage
- disinherited family members or unequal distribution, or
- no living descendants.

Corporate or institutional Trustees have their own pros and cons. They do more, but they also typically cost more. They bring more sophistication and expertise to the table, but can be more rigid and impersonal. They tend to follow the rules strictly (which can be either beneficial or harmful depending on one's perspective). When institutional Trustees are affiliated with or involved in the management of investment assets, they tend to use only those investment options offered on their platform. Many, but not all, institutional Trustees will scrape off the outside advisors, such as the attorney, CPA, or independent investment advisors. Institutional Trustees will generally outlive the people and can fill critical gaps when family members lack financial skills or sophistication.

There are times when an institutional Trustee is absolutely the right choice. Other times, less expensive options get the job done. When selecting a non-family member Trustee, an attorney's professional experience working with potential candidates can give a Grantor useful insights.

A powerful option to consider is a combination arrangement with more than one kind of Trustee. This can provide a best-of-both-worlds solution. For example, a Trust may have a family Trustee who must take the investment advice of a corporate fiduciary or investment advisor. Alternatively, there may be a family Trustee who handles family issues and an institutional Trustee who handles investment decisions. Allocating different areas of control among multiple Trustees can result in a Trust that is stronger and more robust than having all control in a single Trustee.

Any time there is more than one Trustee, it works well to refer to them as a "Board" of Trustees. This structure mirrors the functions and offices of a Board of Directors for a company. If the Trust instrument is drafted appropriately, such a Board can appoint officers such as Managing Trustee, Investment Trustee, or Special Property Trustee and delegate specific duties or responsibilities to such officers. The collective Board can also oversee and provide a safety backstop for individuals serving as a special Trustee with respect to particular businesses or properties, or their own beneficial interests in the Trust.

Another nuanced approach is to designate multiple Trustees, one representing each branch of the family. This structure works particularly well for second marriages or families with stepchildren, where "his" and "her" Trustees can represent each side of the family. Alternatively, a Trustee can represent each child's branch of the family, ensuring that the family lines have representation across generations.

Advanced multi-generational Trusts need to be geared to have and appoint Successor Trustees far into the future beyond the lifespan of all the current parties to the Trust. The Trustee succession provisions of single-use throw-away Trusts are inadequate to sustain and perpetuate the Trust long-term. A well-designed and high-functioning multi-generational Trust will have robust, forward-looking Trustee succession provisions, with multiple mechanisms to ensure that there is always a qualified Trustee.

JURISDICTION INDEPENDENCE

When they got married, Tim and Jill lived in the same town where they grew up. It was idyllic. Life was beautiful for them. They wanted to raise their children in the same place where they had lived all their lives, close to cousins, family, and friends. They had no intention of ever leaving. Then, the real world had its way with them. They found irresistibly good career, business, and family opportunities far from home, in another place. After a long and thoughtful decision-making process, they made the move. Tim and Jill started a new life and created new opportunities in a place they never dreamed of going when they first started out. They and their family thrived in the new location.

Over time, as their family and wealth grew, Tim and Jill expanded their holdings and their relationships even further. They still had a rental home where they had grown up. They also acquired other properties and investments in multiple states. Their children followed suit. They took jobs and pursued business opportunities around the world. The circle of Tim and Jill's influence, property, and family extended far beyond the bounds of where they happened to be living. Without even intending to do so, they found that together with their children, their family and resources were spread out over many locations. They were a multi-jurisdiction family.

After many years of ignoring the sense that updates might be needed, one day, Tim and Jill pulled out the Trust they had set up early in their marriage and reviewed it. They found, to their dismay, that it was tied to a State and its laws where they had not lived for a long time. When they consulted a local attorney where they now lived, the counsel they received was to update their Trust to make it effective where they were then domiciled. On the surface, this sounded reasonable, but Tim and Jill were concerned that they had moved once and may do so again. Now, they own properties and businesses in many places. Their children and grandchildren also lived in many different places. It troubled them that their family and property did not fit neatly into a single location and that tying their estate to one location could lead to confusion and trouble.

Tim and Jill were spot on. Because they lived and worked in multiple places, they saw issues that were not readily apparent to the local attorney, who only did estate planning for clients within the zip code of her office. Tim and Jill wanted a solution that did not lock them into a single jurisdiction that could easily and inadvertently become obsolete.

Tim and Jill were dealing with what might be called "keyhole" legal planning, where the estate plan is viewed through the keyhole of the one state in which the Grantor or the Grantor's attorney happens to live, without seeing the big picture of what is going to happen over time and across jurisdictions. The days of mom, dad, grandad, grandma, and the kids, and perhaps their kids, all living in the same house or even the same community are over. Mobility has consequences for Trust planning. When a Trust is tied to or dependent upon one particular jurisdiction, it becomes immediately obsolete or awkward to administer when the property is acquired elsewhere, and a family member leaves that particular jurisdiction, or the laws in that jurisdiction no longer favor the family.

People move. More than any other time in our history, people, families, and organizations are mobile, highly mobile. If someone is unhappy with their life in Savannah, they can get on the phone or online, find a job, and move to Seattle with an ease undreamed of by our ancestors. But what if the law that governs the family's Trust is immovably fixed to the geographical location of a prior generation who may now be deceased? What if the laws of a particular place no longer serve the family as well as the laws of another place? Is the family stuck despite our society's mobile nature and the law's dynamic nature?

Not necessarily. An "integrated" multi-generational dynasty Trust will account for and accommodate the fact that, especially in today's world, people don't stay put in one place, and over time, their holdings reach far beyond the land of their nativity. A well-crafted Trust can and will allow the domicile of the Trust to move as much and as far as people and assets move. Such a Trust is then independent of any one particular place and may move to different locations from time to time as circumstances warrant. Such a Trust can also function in more than one place at a time. Consider the probability that a Trust will own property in more than one jurisdiction. Weigh the likelihood that a Trust will have Beneficiaries or Trustees in more than one jurisdiction.

The best Trusts are crafted to be portable and jurisdiction-independent. This means they can function in any location and move to a location that best suits the needs and concerns of the parties and the properties over time and across geography.

The best Trusts are crafted to be portable
and jurisdiction-independent.

DOES IT MATTER?

The words that go into your Trust document matter. Who picks the words matters. If you are wise enough to pick your own words, go for it. If you are going to use an advisor to help you choose the words of your Trust, select that advisor by matching the outcome that the advisor will deliver and the outcome that you want. Dramatically different words are required depending on whether or not you just want to avoid probate or you want to protect and preserve your estate from the many hazards that will otherwise impair both your wealth and those who have temporary custody of it.

- Make a written list of what qualifications you want in an advisor who is assisting you with your Trust. Your list may or may not include such things as whether the advisor:

- Builds and maintains their own document templates or outsources them from a third-party provider
- Prepares conveyances to help fund your Trust, such as Deeds for real property and transfers of business entities
- Provides Trust and estate administration services in addition to setting up Trusts
- Has a succession plan to be in business when such services are needed in the future
- Has experience working with a variety of Successor Trustee configurations and both family and non-family Trustees
- Provides you with a mechanism such as Statements of Wishes to add your own words to the Trust beyond those technical words required for the Trust to function.
- If you don't have a Trust, make a list of what you have learned so far in reading this book that will help you determine whether a Trust will be beneficial for you.
- Make another list of some of the features you want to make sure are included in your Trust.
- If you have a Trust and want to do a quick check to determine whether or not it is vulnerable to change by politicians, read it and look for instances where it defers to or relies upon statute rather than laying out its own rules. This is not about setting the Trust's domicile. It's about citing a statute as the ruling authority rather than spelling out an intended rule. It is one thing for a Trust to recite that a particular provision is intended to be in keeping with a statute and another altogether to simply provide that the rules are whatever the statute says.
- Now, look to see where your Trust is domiciled. This is tied to which State's laws govern the Trust, which is related to but different than whether the Trust is built to depend on

State law. Does your Trust give you or someone the ability to change which state's laws govern?

- If your Trust's rules are whatever the applicable statute says they are, you don't fully know what your Trust says. Is that acceptable to you? You are well advised to look up the statutes and read them. If you understand and agree with what the statutes provide, and if you're OK with the idea that the politicians who wrote the statutes can change them, then you may be fine with your Trust as is. Likewise, if your estate is very small and your family is very simple with no issues, and everyone and everything involved in your estate is close to home, a statutory dependent Trust may be a workable fit for you.
- If, on the other hand, you haven't read or don't understand the Trust code, or don't agree with what it states, or are uncomfortable with your Trust being vulnerable to the political process, or your estate is large or your family complicated, or you have family or property in more than one state, it may be time to update and upgrade your Trust.
- If updating or upgrading your Trust is the right move for you, the lawyer who created a statute-dependent Trust for you in the first place may not be the best fit. You can persuade that attorney to do things in a new way and pay for the attorney's education (or pay for what your Trust does or does not do as a result of their lack of experience). Or, it may be time to look for an attorney who already understands that such features as jurisdiction independence and portability are something that should be in a Trust.
- A good clue to whether or not changing out your attorney would be in order is whether or not that attorney has clients outside the zip code and state where his or her office is located. In general, attorneys who regularly work with clients who are dealing with multiple jurisdictions will have already

> developed tools in their practice to accommodate cross-domicile issues. What matters most in this instance is that you have a Trust document and legal counsel that is best suited for your particular needs and circumstances.

These foundations of self-governance reveal the power of a well-crafted Trust. Next, we look at how successful families have applied these principles to create enduring dynasties.

CHAPTER 5

LEARN SUCCESS FROM THE SUCCESSFUL – PRINCIPLES OF ENDURING DYNASTIES

HUNDREDS OF YEARS OF GETTING IT RIGHT

Few people and families have managed to create long-term multi-generational wealth. Most do not. Getting such long-term results never happens by accident. I have been privileged to encounter and work with many families that have built multi-generational wealth that grows in each generation and consistently produces emotionally healthy, highly functional people. Some of these families possess institutional knowledge and wisdom about the opportunities and hazards of multi-generational wealth, which can help us plan more effectively.

Some time ago, I had the privilege of meeting representatives of such a family while attending and speaking at a training event for "Family Offices." This event brought together many ultra-high-income and high-net-worth families from around the world, all united by a common goal: Understanding how to maintain a healthy relationship with their wealth. Many of the speakers and instructors were from long-established, successful families. One individual, who said he was part of the ninth generation of a family enterprise spanning more than two centuries, shared his story with me. His children were part of generation ten, and his grandchildren were generation eleven. They all participated in the substantial financial and familial success, a testament to their shared vision and commitment.

It was enlightening to exchange "war stories" about what works and does not work in such families. We conversed at length about how he and other families had sustained a long line of success over many generations. One of the primary purposes of this book is to share the secrets I have learned through many such conversations.

In this particular case, this gentleman expressed an incredibly wise and insightful view that represented centuries of successful dynasty planning. He told me, "If I want to participate in my family's wealth, I have to help it grow. I don't just get money for being part of the family. I have access to capital, which gives me incredible opportunities. I have amazing connections and experience through my family. I have the use of financial and human resources that are astounding. But I am only able to consume what I produce. My job is to create more wealth than I use for the benefit of those who come after me. The greatest gift my family has given me is the knowledge and experience I need to create my own wealth. We play as a family and enjoy our wealth. But I also get up and work hard every day to give my children and grandchildren that same gift."

He continued. "The mindset in my family is that I don't come to my family with a hat in hand, hoping for a handout. No one gets something for nothing. I don't say, 'I need something, so give me money.' Instead, I come to the table with a plan that I believe will make my family stronger and more secure. What I get from my family is far more than financial. The guidance, ideas, support, and collaboration my family provides turn my good ideas into amazing ideas and amplify my ability to succeed. We don't always agree, but we are always better off working together than working in isolation."

Such an attitude implemented over multiple generations will turn a small amount of wealth into an enormous treasure.

When a member of the extended family needs capital, they have the opportunity to make a pitch, but they have to undergo a vetting and decision-making process. The family doesn't distribute funds willy-nilly just because someone is a relative. The family as a group evaluates the proposal. Is the plan consistent with the family values? Is it economically viable? Is it feasible? Can it work? What are the risks? What are the capital requirements? What are the oversights and safeguards? How will any investment we may make be secured? Where is the family in the capital stack? Will the family be a lender or an equity stakeholder? Will the family get a piece of the upside? Or does the family just get interest? Perhaps most importantly, the family affirmatively provides guidance and counsel to help the proposed deal succeed.

In essence, the family asks the same kinds of questions that a banker would ask before making a loan or that a venture capitalist would ask before putting money into a deal. The man I met had persuaded his family that he had an idea that was worth investing in, and both he and the family shared in the upside. Not only did he have access to the capital and connections needed to put his plan in motion, but he also had direct access to and support from people who knew what they were doing and who had the real-world experience it took for his venture to succeed. From beginning to end, it was a multi-generational collaboration.

Once he had the "go" signal, the family was already in a position to deploy an incredible array of talent and resources. The family functioned like a board of directors to provide counsel, advice, support, and resources. What made family members' advice invaluable was that they had each individually failed, recovered, and succeeded, and they genuinely cared about the success of the new venture. Ironically, if a venture went down in flames, it was viewed as an expensive education that increased the chances for success in the next venture rather than a trigger for shame or disapproval.

A key point in this arrangement was the requirement that he acquire some of the financing on his own, either with his own funds or from outside of the family. The family, as a policy, wouldn't bankroll the entire project. He had to "have skin in the game." It's a basic rule of business that those who have their own resources at risk are far more attentive to taking care of business than someone just using another person's money. Owners behave differently from employees.

From the start, he was miles ahead of any competition. Without a doubt, the process he described was deeply ingrained in his family culture. At the same time, it was made possible because it was built on the foundation of effective dynasty estate planning started centuries ago by people long dead. There were legal structures that correlated with and facilitated the family culture. As a consequence of this long-range vision built into past estate planning, he will not only expand his extended family's assets, but he will also see his own personal wealth grow exponentially during his lifetime. He also sees himself modeling his own estate plan on the same multi-generational approach. He is actively working with the next generation to help them develop the skill set they need to build wealth independently from whatever they might inherit.

Interestingly, although every member of his extended family had the same opportunities and access to capital and resources, every family member applied this to their own degree and in their own way. There were vast differences in the amount of wealth and lifestyle among the various family members. Each person was able to go as far as they wished. Some would hit a comfort level and go no further. Others did more. The contrast in how much wealth individuals created varied among siblings and over generations. Sometimes, the children of one who plateaued at a relatively low level would produce far more wealth than their parents. No one just got something for nothing. But everyone was able to get as much as they were willing to pay the price for.

We discussed at length how his family handled conflict. He noted that they did not always agree or get along, but they were always respectful. This was easier because no one was compelled to be part of anything they did not want to participate in. Some family members had branched out on their own and were pursuing their own ventures without relying on or participating in the family wealth. Sometimes, when the deals were right, there would be cross-investment. But this was never required. He also made the point that having family members doing their own thing outside the family's wealth made the family stronger and gave them more resources to draw upon to further their common goals.

That's multi-generation planning at its best. He made it clear that in his family, this happened by design, on purpose. It wasn't an accident. He could name the ancestors who had started and passed along the process.

On another occasion, I became aware of an investment advisor who made a pitch to a family with "old money." The advisor knew there was a substantial amount of wealth involved, but he did not know how deep the roots went. In any event, he wanted to manage as much of the money as he could. The advisor claimed that his investment strategies included "long-term" investments. The family asked what he meant by "long-term." He boasted that he had investment instruments that lasted as long as ten years.

The family members did not flinch or look at each other. They calmly and kindly said that their "family office" has been in existence for more than 700 years and that "long-term" means at least 200 years for them. Their time horizon was centuries, not decades. They are investing in their great-great-grandchildren, both financially and in terms of family training and culture.

The contrast between those who understand multi-generational dynasty planning and those who do not is striking. An interesting side note: This family is off the public map. You haven't heard of them. One of the skills they have developed in their family is staying out of the spotlight and avoiding unwanted attention and scrutiny. They also steer clear of politics and social engineering. They have plans in place to survive and thrive no matter which way the winds of politics may blow.

A CHECKLIST FOR SUCCESS

Clearly, there are families that have successfully developed a healthy relationship with wealth over multiple generations. Often, we can't tell if an estate plan is successful until time has passed and we are looking back on it.

How can we tell whether an estate plan will work or not going forward? The answer depends on what we define as "success." Does "work" mean that probate was avoided and nothing more? Is "success" just a matter of passing along wealth after a death? Does "success" extend beyond that point in time to include what happens to that wealth generations down the road?

I suggest you consider the following as good indicators that you have succeeded and that your family will continue to succeed as a result of your Trust or estate plan:

- Your wealth goes where you want, and not to the lawyers and the politicians.
- Your beneficiaries are grateful and happy with what you have done, and not resentful or miserable.
- Your wealth makes beneficiaries more productive, not less. They work hard even when they don't have to out of economic necessity.
- Your wealth makes the lives of your beneficiaries more meaningful.

- Your beneficiaries are self-reliant, contributing to society, and improving over time.

If, after a generation or two, your family has chewed itself to pieces, squabbling over and depleting the wealth you worked so hard to obtain, your Trust and estate plan failed. Death-focused estate planning does not even consider or aim for such success.

Such long-term success is the entire focus of dynasty planning. A Dynasty Trust and related structures are specifically intended to address and overcome the overwhelming probability that wealth rarely makes it to or lasts beyond generation three.

FIND THE RIGHT FIT

It is crucial to design a Trust for the specific and long-term goals of the family, setting it up. There are many different kinds of Trusts, numerous options, and a wide variety of tools that may or may not be included in a Trust. Any given type of Trust isn't automatically the best Trust. Even a well-crafted but poorly matched Trust may lead to the opposite of the original goals.

Parents who wish to see the wealth they've earned passed along to future generations have a responsibility to ensure that the transfer is handled in a way that allows their family to persist as a family across multiple generations. If the transfer of wealth ultimately destroys the people, wealth not only has no real value, but it has negative value. The right Trust structure can permit the Beneficiaries to use the assets without allowing them to destroy the assets, and without the wealth destroying the people.

Let's examine some of the possible ways a multi-generational Trust can operate. A Trust can do much more than just avoid probate and pass down wealth. An inherited multi-generational Trust can protect and grow assets in ways that a single-use, self-settled, revocable Trust cannot. This opens up powerful planning opportunities. Rather than simply transferring wealth to the next generation, a Trust can retain the assets under its protective umbrella. Within this protected structure, a Trust may do anything with the assets it owns for the benefit of the family members that the family members could do if they owned the assets personally, including:

- Buy and own properties and assets that the Beneficiaries use and enjoy;
- Make loans to family members to buy homes and businesses and grow their own wealth;
- Form and own businesses that employ family members and increase both the collective and individual wealth of the family members.

When such a Trust is in place for the next generation, they can use the Trust to purchase a house they live in, a car they drive, and perhaps an heirloom property, like a ranch or cabin where the family can spend the summers. When such assets are purchased and owned by a well-structured inherited Trust rather than the family members personally, both the assets and the people are protected from all kinds of potential financial and personal disasters. When structured appropriately, the Trust assets are not available to cover personal liabilities, marital problems, and life dramas of the individuals.

One example of this is structuring the Trust to make loans instead of or in addition to distributions. When a Trust makes loans to family members in lieu of just distributing the money to them, the dynamic changes completely. The inheritance is no longer unearned free money that is available to be used and destroyed by non-productive, self-indulgent life choices. Personal investments of time and work are required. The Trust can require family members to apply for the loan. They will need to say, “Here’s why I need the money, and here’s my collateral.” The Trustees of the Trust can evaluate the situation, set the interest rate, and make the loan if and when it is a healthy and beneficial deal both for the family member and the Trust. Like any other lender, the loan can and should be secured with a lien against appropriate collateral put up by the borrower/Beneficiary, whether a house, business, or investment asset.

A Trust can invest in business enterprises as an alternative to outright distributions. When such a Trust forms a business, invests in a business, or grows a business, it can employ and train the Beneficiaries and family members so that they are equipped and able to run, build, and protect the family empire. Deals can be structured as a joint venture between the Beneficiary and the Trust. This gives the Beneficiary access to capital to create their own wealth, while at the same time growing the collective wealth of the Trust. This can be one of the most powerful aspects of such a Trust.

IT'S NOT THE MONEY; IT'S THE PEOPLE

As generations two, three, four, and so on come on the scene, if the family is functioning effectively and benefiting from the training and experience the family members obtain working in and for the family enterprises, such family members will bring their own market intelligence and business deals to the table. The Family Council becomes a clearinghouse for business ideas and information. When the family is united, prepared, and engaged in growing wealth together, it changes the family dynamic. In addition to having fun and enjoying healthy relationships, when the family gets together, they bring their collective genius and potential business ideas.

- What's happening in the marketplace?
- What are you seeing in your sector or business?
- What are the politicians doing or not doing, and how will it impact us?
- What do we need to safeguard against or take advantage of as the market shifts?

- What new opportunities are there?
- What do you hear or see in the industry sector where you are working?
- What deals or ideas should we look at or consider?

When Generation One integrates the "business of life" and the "life of business" into their Trust and associated business entities while at the same time growing their family, succeeding generations will have learned from a young age how to function like an effective business unit. The family will learn to operate like a board of directors, helping each other individually and the Trust collectively. Family members will come together and decide what deals merit support or help, what dangers to avoid, and how to collaborate for mutual benefit. It becomes a business process rather than a family squabble. The Family Council becomes a business incubator where ideas are introduced, discussed, and evaluated. The family learns to adapt and implement the best ideas.

As a result, the family is not just living off the wealth created by earlier generations, trying to decide how to spend money that someone else earned. Instead, they are actively involved in creating their own wealth based on the foundation set up by prior generations in that Trust. The Trust, therefore, becomes a building block for ongoing success, rather than a stumbling block that destroys initiative and self-reliance.

Building wealth the right way is done only when we remember that money is not the most important thing. It really isn't. The most important thing is the people and how they live their lives. When wealth is created by empowering and helping people live useful, meaningful, and productive lives, and improving the world for the people who live in it, then the price required to obtain the wealth is truly worth it.

DEPENDENCY BREEDS CONTEMPT

When the right multi-generational Trust is put in place, the following generations can become self-reliant rather than dependent. When inherited wealth incapacitates, it is destructive. Dependency breeds contempt. It is sad but common to see second and third generations want, need, demand, live off, and rely on their parents' or grandparents' wealth, and at the same time disrespect and despise the people who provided it.

The inheritors who become self-reliant are the ones who continue to build the dynasty, not the ones who tear it down. It is empowering to say, "I pay my own way. I buy my own groceries. I pay my own rent. I'm not mooching off of Mom and Dad's money. I'm producing my own wealth." These are a different breed of human being, the kind who build rather than merely consume.

The ones who are dependent on others for income, self-esteem, and financial resources become easy targets. Predators lurk in the legal tall grass and wait to strike at some suddenly wealthy person or family. Because these dependent people are spending other people's money and they're living in the shadow of Daddy or Mommy Warbucks, they often retreat to areas of life where they can feel competent. It's a direct effect of dependency. "I can't do that like Grandpa, but I can do this."

Many self-reliant individuals, on the other hand, are able to thrive in creative or entrepreneurial endeavors. Whether they become musicians, playwrights, poets, engineers, designers, scientists, teachers, or entrepreneurs, the fruit of their empowerment benefits both themselves and those around them. Artists and innovators make the world beautiful and functional, and everyone who experiences their contributions is better off. Likewise, some of the greatest innovations in industry and science are made by those who have the leisure and the resources necessary to pursue and create new things. The self-reliant know they can achieve anything, and they often do.

At the same time, the quest for significance in a secondary occupation or avocation can sometimes mask a genuine desire for success somewhere else. When we fail or feel unfulfilled in our family or financial life, success in other pursuits can provide a measure of distraction and relief. But if such substitute pursuits prevent us from achieving real significance, we may be chasing a decoy. When the avocation is a second choice and a way of self-medicating from the pain of not getting what we really want, some self-reflection is warranted. If we ask ourselves what we really want to do, and the answer is "something else," it should give us pause. "I really wanted to do what Grandpa or Grandma did, but I can't, so I'll settle for something else." There's a significant difference between those who pursue creative endeavors because they are otherwise successful and can afford to, and those who settle for second best because that's all they can do.

When people with inherited wealth are not living authentically, they tend to invest in foolish ventures and, as a result, lose their money, family, faith, and any desire to prosper or thrive. When inheritors are in such a negative space, they become the target of predators. There are people whose entire business model is based upon finding that gullible, naive second or third-generation wealth to take advantage of. I've actually had more than one investment fund operator tell me, "Our business model is to look for stupid next-generation people with money because they'll pay us to do things they think they deserve but can't afford and sell us their valuable properties at a deep discount just to get quick cash."

I am reminded of a line from the motion picture The Magnificent Seven. The head bandit, who has been robbing the poor villagers, smiles and says, "If God did not want them sheared, he would not have made them sheep."

Tragically, these vulnerable individuals come to detest their parents and grandparents, blaming them for becoming "sheep to be sheared". Often, their inability to protect themselves can be traced to the way their family's Trust distributed their inherited wealth.

There is a better way.

INDEPENDENCY BREEDS RESPECT

I know a group of successful businessmen who are in their 60s and 70s. They had a rock band when they were much younger. Today, they are professionals and entrepreneurs who have done incredibly well in their careers. They've benefited from family money but have also made a lot of money on their own. And they still have a band. They continue to play at weddings, bar mitzvahs, celebrations, and church parties. I've seen one of their band members spontaneously jump up on a historic stage on Beale Street in Memphis, Tennessee, and, with a borrowed guitar, bring the audience to their feet.

The point is, it's all for fun. They don't need the money. What they need and what they have is the joy of living. Because they have succeeded financially, they can afford the best equipment for their band. They can also afford to charge a higher price for a particular gig or perform for free, depending on the event. They've earned the freedom, and now they're enjoying it. When estate planning actually works, this is the kind of personal success and joy we see in successive generations.

A well-crafted Trust, combined with a high-functioning family, can help the inheritors achieve both financial success and personal fulfillment. Such a structure can provide access to the information and training the next generation needs to succeed, just as the original wealth creators did. With the right attitude, a strong work ethic, and resources provided by a forward-looking Trust, the next generation can succeed both in building wealth and in their personal lives, just like the first-generation wealth builders did.

Regardless of the size of Grandpa's or Grandma's shadow, a Dynasty Trust can give motivated members of future generations the opportunity to step out into their own light. The beauty of this is that as they succeed in creating their own wealth, they can then afford the time and commitment to follow other fields of interest and spend more time with family, all within the framework of financial security.

A well-structured Trust as part of an overall plan for wealth succession and protection can empower future generations to thrive and become their best selves. However, this is only possible if the Trust does not simply hand out money to be wasted. A Trust can help protect the assets by not distributing them. However, for the legal documents to be of any benefit in protecting the people, the family must level up how it functions.

The biggest problem with traditional estate planning is its impact on the individuals and their families. Likewise, the toughest challenge in creating a multi-generational dynasty is how to sustainably prepare and empower the people in the family so that the legacy self-perpetuates. Any multi-generational plan is, by its very nature, a function of the family. No matter how carefully and artfully crafted the legal documents may be, the final outcome for any family will be determined by the character and actions of the people involved.

In decades of helping people think through and plan their estates, I have seen a common thread: Most people care deeply about their family, and they are concerned about what is going to happen to them over time. The prospect of family members dividing up and going through their estate elevates such concerns. Most people also feel that in some way or on some level, their family is messed up and broken. There is no part of building a multi-generational dynastic family that requires a trouble-free, perfect family. To the contrary, the point is that with the help of the right tools, we can set in motion a family and wealth dynamic that will thrive over time in spite of the enormous variety of human failings that we all deal with.

Every one of the families I have encountered with a history of or potential for multi-generational prosperity has been different.

Every family will have its own traditions and its own culture. Each will have its own challenges and hardships. No family is mistake-free or without its own drama. Every family will be recovering from something. Wherever your family is at now and no matter what you may be going through, it does not preclude setting in motion the processes that will bring about high-functioning multi-generational stability.

* * *

Although it may go by different names, there is a common function that consistently occurs within long-lasting families. There is one specific mechanism that will enable your family to overcome any challenge it may face. Of all the things that you could potentially do to prepare your family to be good at multi-generational planning, there is one course of action in particular that a family leader can implement that will produce one of the most significant and lasting benefits: holding family council.

Any time family members gather or communicate with each other about any matter that concerns the family, it is a family council. For most of us, most of the time, such communication is accidental or merely incidental to going through the motions that being a family imposes upon its members. I am suggesting that the family council function become a deliberate and intentional component of the family culture and tradition. I am suggesting that every member of the family take ownership of the family council concept and not only affirmatively participate, but also do what it takes to make it happen.

A family council can be informal or formal, spontaneous or regularly scheduled, ad hoc or scripted with an agenda. The free-form, unplanned family councils will be more effective and beneficial if they are accompanied by regularly occurring, structured, pre-planned family councils. Such a formal family council may include some or all of the following:

- There should be a written agenda outlining what will happen in the council meeting.
- The persons presiding or in charge of the meeting are generally the most senior members of the family present at the meeting, Mom and Dad or the grandparents. They may ask various family members to contribute to the council meeting, or they may delegate this to the person conducting the meeting.
- A family member should be asked in advance to conduct or run the council meeting. The person who conducts the meeting typically also puts together the agenda and asks family members to participate in the various functions. Over time, every member of the family, young and old, should be given the opportunity to have this role. Children and adults alike who have experience and know how to plan and conduct a meeting will have a significant advantage over their peers.
- The family should develop or adopt their own tradition for an opening ceremony. This might include a song or hymn, prayer, meditation, recitation of a scripture verse or family theme, or an inspirational thought.
- A family member should be asked in advance to teach or give instructions on a preplanned topic. This can cover any idea or concept that will benefit the family. It can be based on a book or a class that a family member is attending. It can be like the family's private TED Talk. Again, every member of the family, young and old alike, should be given an opportunity to prepare and teach. This, too, will give family members

significant advantages in school, the business world, and life in general.

- The agenda may include games, entertainment, musical or poetic recitals, or other forms of sharing family members' talents and simply having fun together.
- The family may acknowledge and celebrate birthdays, anniversaries, graduations, accomplishments, and events. It may work well to give each family member an opportunity to report on what is going on in their lives so that family members are aware of and connected with each other.
- Family councils are a perfect place to address and make family decisions, goals, and plans. Whether it's a question of how to spend a holiday, career changes, educational options, moving, homework, what's for dinner, or your estate plan, every aspect of family life can be thought through and determined in council and by counseling with family members. When family members participate in the decision-making process, the quality of the decisions will improve, and the family will be more motivated and better equipped to deal with where the decision leads.
- Over time, through the family council process, the family should discuss and consider its mission, vision, and purpose. These should be rendered into written statements or themes that the family recites and integrates into daily life.
- As needed, time and resources should be set aside for family members to safely, respectfully, and honestly address and resolve conflict and disagreement. The probability of conflict in a family is 100%. Don't be surprised or disappointed by it. Rather, view it as an opportunity. Some of the most beautiful music is made when dissonance

resolves. Without the dissonance, the beauty of resolution does not happen.

- Time or specific meetings should be set aside to specifically deal with family business. On one level, this may simply be the business of life, jobs, sickness, moving, relationships, and practical everyday needs. On another level, this should be dealing with the family's business, professional, commercial, and economic activities. This element of the family council should be as rigorous and comprehensive as the board meeting of any major corporate enterprise. This particular function of the family council should also be appropriately documented with particular attention to decisions made, follow-through action items of the participants, and details needed for corporate or tax compliance purposes.

The family should develop or adopt their own tradition for a closing ceremony, perhaps with a benediction or blessing and a treat.

The most important thing is the people and how they live their lives

The ability to plan and conduct effective business meetings is one of the fundamental skill sets required to succeed in business. It is surprising that so many successful business people who do this well at the office don't apply the same skills in their family. Success in business and success in the family should not be mutually exclusive. They should be complementary. Being good at one should help us be good at the other. In my experience, if we first learn how to be good at this in the family, being good at it in business happens naturally. Those families that successfully implement a multi-generational plan know that for the high-quality legal documents they pay for to be of any benefit, the family has to work. Such work and high function begin and are sustained through the family council.

It is a fundamental attribute of the decision-making process that decisions made in consultation with parties who have a vested stake in the outcome will be better than those made in isolation. It is worth noting that as the family builds trust and confidence in each other and in the family council process, the family council becomes a tremendous resource for family members both individually and as a group to counsel. The safest and most effective place for people to receive counsel as we all work through life's challenges can and should be the family. We learn to counsel with each other in council.

There is no substitute for effective family leadership. Professional advisors can't do it for you. The nanny, the lawn guy, and the domestic help can't do it for you. You have to step up and be the leader. Building a family and a family culture that embodies the ambitious ideas and principles described in this book is no small undertaking. I encourage you to dig in and study what it takes to bring your family to a place where multi-generational dynasty planning will be a realistic expectation. Implement and develop the family council, and help every family member get good at it on purpose.

The most important thing is the people and how they live their lives.

DOES IT MATTER?

Some time ago, in a craft store, I saw a sign that read, "Families Are Forever." This phrase can have many layers of meaning that go beyond the purpose of this book. One important meaning is that families are self-replicating. We reproduce both biologically and economically. There are families that die out and have no issue, and families that persist and spread until their descendants fill the earth. In a Darwinian sense, it is survival of the fittest. So, a forever family is the family that survives and thrives.

All the money in the world cannot replace a broken family, but a high-functioning family can acquire all the money it ever needs. If we start with the family, the legal and financial planning will be effective. If we expect a Trust or any other legal document or structure to do the difficult family side of the work for us, we will be disappointed.

If this chapter resonated with you, here are some suggestions:

- Write down in your own words a list of what you would like your family to look like and how you would like it to function when every living person in your family right now is gone and your family is comprised completely of people who have not yet been born.
- Study families and individuals who have attained what you want for you and your family. Read their biographies and histories. Examine and think through what made them tick and how they made decisions. Look at how long and how well the success lasted. Learn from those who blew it and lost it as well as from those who have kept it going.
- Think of one family, institution, or organization that has sustained excellence across multiple generations. What specific practices or principles made that possible? Which of those could you adopt or adapt for your own family?
- Hold a formal family council.
- These principles of enduring success show us what's possible. Next, we explore how to build the integrated system that makes it happen.

Family councils are the living heartbeat that turns principles into practice. They build the human capital that no legal document can create on its own: trust, communication, shared purpose, leadership. But Family Councils alone are not enough. To truly sustain multi-generational prosperity, the family needs structures that match the strength of its people. That is where the next chapter begins: moving from the council table to the integrated systems that give councils real power to govern and grow wealth across time: Dynasty Trusts, a Family Office, Family Bank, a Family Foundation and related charitable vehicles. The infinite game requires both: strong players and a strong playing field.

Turn the page to see how to build the field.

CHAPTER 6

INTEGRATED DYNASTY TRUST REVOLUTION – BUILDING THE SYSTEM

FROM TRUST TO INTEGRATED DYNASTY

A "dynasty" is intended to outlive its creators. For the purposes of this book, I refer to a Trust designed with forward-thinking features, along with related structures and processes aimed at protecting and expanding wealth across multiple generations, as an "Integrated Dynasty Trust." This is not just a single, standalone Trust; it necessarily involves additional components. Understanding how this Trust interconnects with other essential planning elements is crucial.

Building your own "dynasty" starts with having a plan that goes beyond your lifetime and addresses more than just what you now possess or those who are now living. In structuring such a plan, it is essential to bring to bear a full array of tools to optimize the probability that your plan will become a reality when you are no longer present to monitor its progress.

The basketball film Hoosiers features a coach who continually advised his team to "wait for the good shot." That same principle applies in estate planning. While it's true that having any Will or

Trust is better than having none, after all, you can't score if you never shoot, indiscriminately taking any shot isn't wise.

A Trust or Will is ineffective if not crafted with strategic planning tailored to the family's specific needs and circumstances, considering all the players' positions on the court, and recognizing the true nature of "the game." There is no point in scoring a point now (taking and hitting one shot) if we lose the game (destroying the money and/or the family) at any point in the future.

THE DYNASTY GAME PLAN

Effective estate planning isn't a zero-sum or finite game where the end goal is merely to declare a winner upon someone's passing. Instead, to be effective, the plan must be viewed as one element of an infinite game, focusing on continuity and sustainability rather than just asset distribution at the end. A scarcity mindset, where estate planning devolves into determining who gets what upon death, fosters conflict and is counterproductive.

Viewing estate planning as a finite game blinds us to crucial aspects of what is happening over time. The fact is that for as long as time has been measured, there have been people and property, but the particular people and property consistently change. They both ebb and flow in an unending stream. Most of us have difficulty thinking about any part of that stream other than our own. We only see our own time and our own assets. We rarely look back to see how generations past have brought us to where we are now. We don't see how what we do now is going to change things beyond our own limited time in mortality.

To the extent that we don't see or take into consideration the whole picture, our plans will be incomplete and flawed. If we don't see things as they really are, our plans cannot be effective. Our estate plans are only effective when they account for and address such immutable facts of life.

Thus, to be effective, an estate plan must be viewed and treated as a team event in an infinite game. Such a plan goes beyond merely covering the whole field of play for one isolated game. It reaches beyond a strategy to win every game for an entire season. Such a plan will be built on the recognition that the game continues in a never-ending flow. So, we will develop patterns of preparation and training to maximize the number of wins forever.

The team members (family) and the object of play (wealth or prosperity) and the referees (laws) will unavoidably change over time, but the game never terminates. A single star player making one good shot in one game might look good for a fleeting moment, but it doesn't win the unending game. Those who win the infinite game look beyond one good shot today. Being the leader in an effective estate plan is not about your good shot now, but all the good shots yet to come that will be made by others.

In part, the infinite game estate plan will be a function of how well your planning is integrated with your family, business, and the rest of the universe. To be integrated and not just a one-person team taking one shot against an imposing opposition, a Trust must have certain structures and components and own certain assets. It cannot be an isolated pile of paper in a notebook tucked away in your closet. It must be an active part of a larger picture.

BUILDING THE TEAM AND THE PLAYING FIELD

Too often, otherwise good planning leaves gaps in protection and outcome because there is little or no connection between the business and property structures and the estate structures, or because the accounting, legal, investment, and insurance advisers, as well as family members, are each doing their own thing without coordinating with one another. The best players who can't or won't work together as a team will consistently be defeated by high-functioning teams that come to a particular game prepared to win the season, knowing what the real game and winning actually are, having a strategy, and the resources needed to prevail. A ragtag bunch of individual hot shots doing their own thing in a disconnected fashion with no cohesive governance, no matter how talented, smart, and virtuous such individuals may be, may look good for one play or one game, but are less likely to win season after season.

What I call an Integrated Dynasty Trust will be "integrated" when it is combined with and connected to the people and other business structures such as, where appropriate, a "Family Office" management company to protect and segregate control, a "Family Bank" asset and equity holding company to insulate risk from value, and a "Family Foundation" to build influence and capture and repurpose wealth otherwise lost through taxation, and "Special Purpose Entities" to hold and operate particular assets, properties, and operations.

Setting up integrated structures and components also requires the advisors to function as a team and not as independent players "doing their own thing" to the detriment of the desired outcome which is team victory in the infinite game. When implementing an Integrated Dynastic Trust, the building materials that go into it, how they are assembled, and what we do with them can help produce consistent, repeated victories in the infinite game.

The probability of change over time in a family and in finances is one hundred percent. The very definition of time is change. It cannot be avoided so long as we inhabit this mortal world. Whether or not the old adage that "the more things change, the more they stay the same" applies is often a function of foresight and perspective, particularly in estate planning. Change can, without a doubt, be anticipated and managed. Traditional death-oriented planning simply dumps property on the next generation with no tools to address the inevitable change that accompanies a sudden increase in wealth. When a Trust is designed with multi-generational succession in mind, channeling change in a healthy direction becomes an integral part of the plan.

SEEING THE FUTURE IN THE PAST

The unpredictable and unknown acts of present and future family members, competitors, predators, and politicians can dramatically affect your estate plan, so such factors must be considered when developing that plan and Trust. No one can accurately predict all the creative ways politicians will come up with to levy taxes. But when planning for anything that will outlive us, such as our estate, experience teaches us that there are tools that can be deployed to accommodate and anticipate the inevitable change.

Imagine a person who has never driven any kind of car before or had any instruction on how to do so, getting behind the wheel of a high-performance vehicle loaded with people and valuables and attempting to drive at high speeds on a freeway. Operating a Trust with no experience or understanding of what it does and how it works is no different.

When financially illiterate people are put in charge of what happens with the money, it can be catastrophic. To prevent the change from going in an unproductive direction, it is crucial that family members have financial responsibility and accountability early on so that they learn what works. It is also crucial to provide guidance on what kind of changes should be made.

The film A Few Good Men features a great line from the Jack Nicholson character, Col. Jessup, who is interrogated by an attorney who wants to hear the truth. Jessup shouts, "You can't handle the truth!" That statement sums up an uncomfortable fact about some Beneficiaries. They can't handle the truth of sudden wealth. In particular, they can struggle to distinguish beneficial change from harmful change. They tend to view potential change through the keyhole perspective of what gives them the most pleasure in the moment.

I have encountered this sad situation many times. For example, I worked with a man I will call Stan who was the Beneficiary of an enormous sum of money. He received an annual annuity check at the beginning of every year. For several years prior to coming to our firm, within three days of getting that check, all the money was gone. He spent wildly on prostitutes, gambling, and drugs. Stan never invested a penny in creating anything positive in his life. He personified the lyrics of an old Doors song: "I want the world, and I want it now!"

For some reason which I could not discern, Stan thought of himself as a financial genius. He wanted all the money at once. "I can take it and invest it and make more money than the lump sum I get every year. Yeah, I can do that!" He came to the law firm I was in at the time for help with breaking the annuity. I remember personally counseling him. "Don't do this. This is a bad idea." He was adamant. "No, no, no, I want to do this. I can handle it."

At Stan's insistence, the firm took the case to court and a judge approved collapsing the annuity. In spite of my concerns, the firm concluded that, having given him the benefit of our counsel, once he made the decision, our role was to carry it out. It was, as predicted, a stupid financial move. Stupid is a harsh word, but it's accurate in describing a financial move that guaranteed a massive negative rate of return. Without delay, he continued on the same path of losing money left and right. He made one so-called investment that was in reality a giant gamble. The gamble worked against him, and he quickly blew what was left of the sudden influx of wealth in amazingly foolish ways.

Once the money was gone, Stan had no income and had to find work. However, his capacity for work was diminished by the abusive lifestyle he had been living. Today, this self-styled financial whiz, who was wealthy beyond most people's dreams, has no fortune. His wife and kids left him. He's working a menial job and living paycheck-to-paycheck. Not long ago, he stopped by my office without an appointment because of a small legal issue. I wish I could report how many years he has been sober. But I can't. He continues to pay the price.

Examples of unearned wealth spoiling or even ruining the lives of the Beneficiaries are legendary. Most millionaires in America are self-made in one generation. They have a tremendous work ethic and have sacrificed throughout their lives to achieve the wealth they have earned. Whether the Grantor is a millionaire or someone with assets below that benchmark, the last thing anyone wants is for their wealth to ruin the upcoming generations. This is especially true of those who have a strong work ethic and believe that all of us should be productive members of society.

Sad stories like Stan's are endlessly repeated in part because death and money-oriented estate planning does not account for the people and provide them with values that guide what kind of changes they should implement. Contrast Stan's experience with someone who had a better foundation upon which to base financial decisions.

HOPE BURNS BRIGHTLY

Some years ago, I worked with the "next generation" of a very wealthy family. They were faced with a business decision involving millions of dollars, and only two options were on the table. One would immediately put millions of dollars in the pockets of the next generation of family members. The other would cost the family members a lot of money, but would provide millions of dollars in benefits to the employees of a family-owned business.

The discussion was highly animated. I was one of at least three attorneys in the room. There were also two or three accountants, several business consultants, and a number of financial advisors for the family. The general consensus from the crowd of advisors was the same: Take the money. It seemed to be the obvious move that anyone would make. The advisors were surprised when the family pushed back.

As the pitch of the discussion rose, "Carmen", the family's eldest daughter, waved everyone to their seats. By her skill and her wit, among all her siblings, Carmen had ascended to lead the family businesses after her parents passed. She pulled a photocopy of some handwritten pages from her briefcase, and I knew what they were the minute I saw them. I had discussed the contents of these pages in depth with her father years earlier, and I was with him when he put his thoughts to paper.

She read out loud a section from her father's "Statements of Wishes." He told the story of how he and his wife had started their first company. He spoke of their sacrifices. He told of not having enough money to afford a hotel and spending nights sleeping in his car away from his children. Carmen remembered those nights; He recounted how, from the very beginning of the business, he and his wife had decided to pay their employees before they paid themselves. They had always made it a priority to invest in the people who worked for their company.

Then he said that when it came time to sell that business, it had so much value because of the hard work and loyalty of the many employees who labored in the business. By investing in the people and ensuring their needs were met before they took money out of the business for themselves, they made the business successful, which returned a huge dividend when that business eventually sold. The sale of that first company launched a string of new business ventures that Carmen was now leading and growing, and there were now substantially more employees.

Carmen then said, in effect, that "The decision is obvious. This is not about how much money the family members can take out of the business. This is about taking care of the people who are doing the work in the company. We will grow this company by investing in the people who are doing the work, just like our parents did. That is best for the Company, for its employees, and our family."

So, the advisors' consensus was ignored. That business enterprise has continued to grow and prosper and is giving a growing number of families, not just the next generation of owners, the ability to thrive.

LOADING THE TOOLBOX

The intention and benefit of an integrated plan will be realized only when the people carrying out the plan have the best available tools when and where they need them, and they know how to use the tools effectively. This requires:

- Logistical Preparation: Ensuring the tools are available when and where needed involves structuring the Trust and related components correctly from the outset. This is analogous to making sure that the right ladder is available when and where the team members need it.
- Tactical Knowledge: Future generations must be educated in using these tools, involving them early in wealth management and Trust operations. This involves both present leadership and training future leaders to ensure that the family and their advisors act cohesively. This is analogous to making sure that everyone on the team knows which ladder they are climbing and how to climb it effectively.
- Strategic Deployment: Everyone on the team must know not only the common objective but also what that objective should be and what their role is in accomplishing it. This is about optimizing what actually works best as opposed to things that should not exist. It is analogous to making sure that the ladder is on the right wall.

Every person and family is unique, and these differences evolve. An effective multi-generational Trust must accommodate these variations, not only for the present, but also anticipating an unknown future. In the infinite game of dynasty planning, a Trust should be tailored with a broad array of tools to serve multiple generations. Eons after their invention, we still use wheels today in ways never imagined in the past. When we put such metaphorical wheels on the Trusts we establish today, they become resources future family members will be able to use to solve problems we haven't even thought of yet.

When we anticipate using a Trust over multiple generations, it becomes increasingly important to load the Trust up with tools that might be useful someday, even if they are not needed in the present moment.

For example, it may be that at this time, a family has no incapacitated or special needs people. That could easily change with the next generation. Odds are that one in five families will have a special needs individual within two generations. We just don't know in advance which family. A "Special Needs Trust" provides for a special needs individual without jeopardizing other benefits the individual may be entitled to, and can protect assets from any vulnerabilities and liabilities of the individual. Typically, in the absence of an immediate need, such special needs tools are left out of most Trusts. If or when the need arises, it triggers additional costs, and the add-on solutions are more cumbersome and awkward. It is better to simply include special needs provisions in the Trust from the start so that the tool is available if and when it is needed.

Because there are many factors that we just don't know, and the future is ridiculously hard to predict, it makes sense to load up the toolbox so that future generations are prepared for and have the resources to deal with the unforeseen. Adequate tools for the job, including unknown future jobs, should be available in the toolbox. It's just common sense to build into the Trust tools to address future issues, both seen and unseen.

Such emergency tools may be analogous to the safety equipment on a car. If a vehicle is used over its economic life and the seat belts, airbags, anti-lock brakes, spare tire, and other emergency equipment are never deployed, it just means the driver and passengers got lucky. The tools are there to deal with emergencies, whether or not they actually happen, because they can and will happen sometimes. And even if you never use the airbag, just knowing that it's in place not only provides significant peace of mind, it optimizes safety in the event of an accident.

It is important to note that loading up a Trust with tools for future use is not governing from the grave. The first person who crafted a wheel and attached it to a wagon did not pre-determine where or how you are going to drive your car. Building in tools for future use does not make decisions in advance. Rather, it equips future generations with resources to assess each situation as it arises and respond in a manner that is most appropriate and effective.

An "integrated" Trust, designed with a long-term perspective, will have a full array of tools, which may include:

- Principal Protection: Mechanisms to safeguard and grow wealth over time rather than permitting it to be distributed and consumed.
- Dispute Resolution: Built-in methods for resolving conflicts efficiently without resorting to litigation.
- Trust Protector: A party to both keep the Trust on track with the Grantor's intent and adjust Trust terms as unexpected circumstances arise.
- Tax Planning: Flexibility to allocate tax liability to the most efficient taxpayer.
- Perpetuity Provisions: Enabling the Trust to exist indefinitely.
- Jurisdictional Flexibility: The ability to move the Trust to more favorable legal environments.
- Special Needs Provisions: Tools to provide and care for Special Needs family members without clobbering their other benefits.

- Generation-Skipping: To reduce or eliminate taxation with the passing of each generation.
- Addiction and Gambling Safeguards: Protecting assets from misuse and abuse.
- Legislative Contingency: A "Congressional Ambush Recovery Plan" to adapt to new laws or tax policies.

This list is not exhaustive but serves as a warning. The only certainty in law, the market, and life is change. Therefore, adaptability is key. The Trust's ability to protect and help the family in the future will depend upon mechanisms to incorporate new tools and/or adjust existing ones as the legal and economic landscapes evolve.

MANAGING CHANGE

The probability of change over time in a family and in finances is one hundred percent. The very definition of time is change. It cannot be avoided so long as we inhabit this mortal world. Whether or not the old adage that "the more things change, the more they stay the same" applies is often a function of foresight and perspective, particularly in estate planning.

Change can, without a doubt, be anticipated and managed. Traditional death-oriented planning simply dumps property on the next generation with no tools to address the inevitable change that accompanies a sudden increase in wealth. When a Trust is designed with multi-generational succession in mind, channeling change in a healthy direction becomes an integral part of the plan.

Some years ago, while on a trip to Egypt, our guide pointed out a massive obelisk covered with hieroglyphics. He said, "Let me translate this for you." Then he proceeded to tell us that this giant stone said that all the land from where we stood to the edge of the Nile River belonged tax-free to some ancient person (whose name I could not pronounce and do not remember) and his descendants in perpetuity forever. Thinking that this sounded a lot like a multi-generational Dynasty Trust, I asked where the descendants of this person were. The guide replied, "No one knows. They have all been dead for thousands of years."

The lesson is stark: even the most ambitious perpetual arrangements eventually crumble when they cannot adapt to time, politics, mobility, or unforeseen change. That is exactly why an Integrated Dynasty Trust must be built for evolution, not just endurance.

The unpredictable and unknown acts of present and future family members, competitors, predators, and politicians can dramatically affect your estate plan, so such factors must be considered when developing that plan and Trust. No one can accurately predict all the creative ways politicians will come up with to levy taxes. But when planning for anything that will outlive us, such as our estate, experience teaches us that there are tools that can be deployed to accommodate and anticipate the inevitable change.

The intention and benefit of an integrated plan will be realized only when the people carrying out the plan have the best available tools when and where they need them, and they know how to use the tools effectively.

DOES IT MATTER?

- Envision your family thriving 50, 100, or even 200 years from now. What specific outcomes would make you proud: sustained wealth growth, strong relationships, meaningful contributions to society, self-reliant and fulfilled descendants?
- Have you ever mapped out your family's wealth and decision-making structures on paper (Trust(s), business entities, Family Office, Family Bank, charitable vehicles)? If not, sketch a simple diagram this week; what gaps appear when you look at it through the lens of 50 or 100 years?

- Does your plan assume today's laws, tax rules, family locations, and investment options will still be favorable decades from now? What single change (new tax law, family move, market shift) could most threaten it, and what adaptability tools (Trust Protector powers, situs flexibility, perpetuity provisions) are missing?
- Are future generations already being taught how to use the "toolbox" you're building (loans instead of gifts, incentives for productivity, board-style governance)? If not, what is one small way you can begin that education now, perhaps a family council discussion or sharing one principle from this chapter?
- Have you assembled (or planned to assemble) a true integrated advisory team (attorney, CPA, financial planner, perhaps a family-business consultant) that meets regularly and speaks the same language about dynasty goals, not just annual tax filings? If the team is fragmented, what is your next step to align them?
- When you picture the infinite game, your great-grandchildren facing decisions you can't foresee today, do you feel confident they will have both the financial capital **and** the human capital (character, skills, unity) to thrive? What one feature can you add to your plan right now to strengthen that human side?
- What legacy do you want your family to celebrate about your choices, not just the size of the estate, but the strength and purpose of the people who inherit it?
- If GST (Generation-Skipping Transfer) tax exclusion is allocated, are Trust-owned assets explicitly kept out of Beneficiaries' taxable estates? How much could your family preserve tax-free over 50-100 years if the wealth compounds inside the Trust instead of being taxed at each generation?

- Looking at the contrast between the traditional outright-transfer path (losing billions to taxes) and the GST-exempt dynasty path (zero transfer taxes), which future do you want for your descendants? What one change can you make now to move closer to the Dynasty model? See "The Dynasty Contrast" on page 132
- What is one concrete, realistic step you can take **this month** to move your plan from "estate documents" toward "integrated dynasty system"?

The tools and mindset of integration lay the groundwork. Next, we examine the critical safeguard that keeps the system on course: the Trust Protector.

CHAPTER 7

PROTECTOR PROTECTION – THE FOURTH PARTY SAFEGUARD

THE FOURTH PARTY MISSING IN ACTION

As we noted at the beginning of the book, three parties are required to form a Trust: a Grantor, a Trustee, and a Beneficiary. Someone, presumably the Grantor, must also convey assets to the Trust for it to come into existence.

To protect a Trust, there are certain functions which are best performed by a fourth party, which has come to be called a Trust Protector. In some Trusts, the Trust Protector may go by another title, such as Special Trustee, Limited Trustee, or similar terms. A Trust without a Protector is a Trust ill-equipped to deal with the various risks that Trusts inevitably encounter over time. Think about all those Western TV shows where the marshal or sheriff is dead or out of town, and the community is plundered by predators riding in from the prairie. The world is full of predators that will eventually strike any Trust. The unprotected Trust and its parties will be the most severely affected.

THE PROTECTOR'S POWERS

The Grantor may give the Trust Protector certain specified and enumerated powers and authority regarding the Trust and its administration. These powers are different from those of a Trustee and generally do not include holding assets. As determined by the Grantor in the Trust instrument, these powers may be very broad or narrow.

The Protector's authority may include the power to remove or replace Trustees and Beneficiaries, cure ambiguities, modify terms and conditions of the Trust, resolve disputes, and interpret or enforce provisions of the Trust instrument.

A typical power given to the Protector is the ability to modify the provisions of the Trust to comply with changes in the law or to recover from a "tax ambush," which can happen when politicians change the rules that apply to a Trust after it has become irrevocable.

Often, a Protector will also have the power to make elections or discretionary determinations where other parties are otherwise barred from doing so due to conflicts of interest. For example, a Protector may have the power to approve or disapprove a loan or distribution from the Trust to a Beneficiary who is also a Trustee, where such a Trustee/Beneficiary would not be permitted to make such a loan or distribution to themselves. This permits the Trust to provide for the Beneficiaries while protecting both the Trust and the Beneficiaries from predators and from themselves. Notably, in such a scenario, the Protector does not make the loan or handle the Trust assets. The Protector reviews the transaction and approves or disapproves based on compliance with applicable law and the governing terms of the Trust.

The language of the Trust will generally determine the Protector's powers. In some instances and jurisdictions, a Protector's powers may also be limited or supplemented by statute or by judicial decision. Some think that a Trust Protector is a relatively new development.

In fact, it is not. At the same time, the scope, extent, and variety of the Trust Protector's powers are evolving and will continue to evolve.

WHO APPOINTS THE PROTECTOR?

The terms of the Trust may permit the Protector to be appointed by the Grantor, certain Trustees, or certain Beneficiaries. In most revocable Trusts, the Grantor will appoint the Protector and will have the power to replace or change the Protector while living. Because such Trusts are amendable by the Grantor, as long as the Grantor is living, the Protector will not do anything or have any real power. While living, the Grantor will do what a Protector might otherwise do. When the Grantor dies and the Trust becomes irrevocable, the Trust Protector plays a vital role in preserving the purpose and function of the Trust.

With an irrevocable Trust, the Grantor will typically also appoint the initial Protector. The Grantor may or may not retain the direct or indirect power to change the Protector even with an Irrevocable Trust. There can be nuanced tax consequences if the Grantor retains certain controls over the Trust, so the Grantor's retained power has to be carefully structured so that it does not rise to a "power of appointment" that would cause the irrevocable Trust to be included in the Grantor's taxable estate or available to the Grantor's creditors.

The big question is, who has the power to appoint or remove a Trust Protector when the Grantor is no longer living and available to perform that function?

The party with the power to appoint a Protector has far-reaching consequences. This is because the Protector typically acts as a check and balance to ensure that the Trust's terms are followed and that the parties to the Trust comply with its terms and conditions. The party with the power to appoint, remove, or replace the Protector will be able to require the Protector's loyalty. A party that may be held accountable by the Protector should never be the one to appoint the Protector.

For example, consider the Protector's power to remove a Trustee who is in some fashion not complying with the terms of the Trust or fulfilling the Trustee's duties and obligations. If the Protector has the power to remove a Trustee and the Trustee has the power to remove the Protector, which power prevails? Likewise, if the Protector has the power to remove a Beneficiary who wrongfully brings a lawsuit against the Trust, and the Beneficiary also has the power to remove the Protector, again, which power prevails?

In granting whatever powers the Protector may or may not have and deciding how and on what conditions a Protector is named or replaced, the priorities of such powers must be addressed. This is one of the reasons why it is generally best that the Protector NOT be a fiduciary. The Protector's loyalty should ultimately be to the Grantor and to implementing the Grantor's intent in the Trust. So, if that includes refusing to approve a distribution to a Beneficiary dealing with an addiction, the Protector's power should triumph over the Beneficiary's right to get money out of the Trust.

WHO QUALIFIES?

It is perhaps easier to identify who should not be the Protector than who should be the Protector. Some people mistakenly think that a party easily controlled or manipulated is best. Giving the powers of a Trust Protector to a person who lacks the life experience or judgment to protect themselves or the Trust creates more problems than it might solve. Good ol' cousin Bob might be considered a good (patsy) candidate because the family knows he will just do what he is told, and they can push him around. But if the entire family so easily manipulates Bob, he's probably just as easily manipulated by any one member of the family. Suddenly, it's Bob and whoever pushes hardest at the moment against the rest of the family. Chaos follows.

When an advisor floats the idea that a cousin, uncle, or aunt could be named the Protector because they will do what they are told, you should run away. Even sophisticated and highly educated individuals can find the subtleties and nuances of Trust law and taxation daunting. Throw in the pressures from individual and collective family members, and you'll create a potentially disastrous situation. Select your Trust Protector with care.

The Protector should also not be one of the other parties to the Trust, such as a Grantor, Trustee, or Beneficiary. Giving those parties the powers of a Protector can have adverse consequences. For example, if the Grantor has the powers of the Protector with an irrevocable Trust, the assets of the Trust have a high risk of being included in the taxable estate or available to the creditors of the Grantor. If the Beneficiaries have such powers, the creditors of the Beneficiary could compel the use of such powers to subvert the Trust and take its assets. If the Trustee has such powers, the checks and balances are unhinged.

It is generally best for the Trust Protector to be a neutral third-party with no beneficial or economic interest in the estate. Due to the level of judgment and discretion required, the best candidates for the Protector are licensed professionals such as an attorney, CPA, or someone with similar credentials and training. Licensed professionals not only have training and experience that aid in performing the Protector's function, but they are also subject to independent licensing and ethical requirements that help keep them from misbehaving. Lawyers and CPAs will do many things for their clients, but breaking the law and losing their professional credentials is generally not one of them.

Sometimes, it works well for the Protector to be a council or group of more than one person. For example, the Protector "committee" or "counsel" could be comprised of an attorney, a CPA, and a financial advisor. This mitigates the potential for a single individual to be manipulated or subject to group pressure. It also then gives the Trust the benefit of the expertise of multiple complementary disciplines. If more than one person must sign on to the Protector's action, it can reduce the chances of getting off track. The downside of this approach is that the more people involved in the process, the more it will cost and the longer it will take to make decisions. The tradeoff is sometimes worth it with very large or complex estates.

The bottom line is that choosing the wrong Trust Protector can accomplish the opposite of what having a Protector should accomplish.

PROTECTOR CHECKS AND BALANCES

The Protector serves as a check and a balance. What if the Protector misbehaves? There is a valid need to protect the Trust from the Protector's inappropriate conduct. Several measures may be implemented to prevent abuse by the Trust Protector, including:

- Prohibit the Protector from taking possession of Trust assets. Taking custody of Trust assets can turn the Protector into a fiduciary. If the Protector is a fiduciary, it is crucial to identify who is entitled to the Protector's loyalty (the Grantor, the Trustee, the Beneficiary, the politicians, or the tax collector?). Misplaced duty may impair the Protector's ability to carry out the Grantor's intent or to protect the Trust from a bad actor. In most instances, the Protector's loyalty should be to the Grantor and the Grantor's intent as spelled out in the Trust, not to the Beneficiaries or the Trustee. The Trust instrument may expressly determine whether or not the Protector is a fiduciary, and if the Trust is silent on that point, it may be determined by local statute or the courts.
- Prohibit the Protector from naming themselves, their estate, or their heirs as Beneficiaries or Trustees and from "appointing" any of the Trust assets for their benefit.
- Carefully distinguish between what the Protector can and cannot do unilaterally. This means certain Protector actions

must either be invoked by parties to the Trust or done with their consent. For example, certain actions, such as removing a bad Trustee or modifying the terms of the Trust to comply with changes in tax law, may require the consent of other parties.

- Identify how conflicting powers are to be resolved. For example, if the Trustee can remove the Protector and the Protector can remove a Trustee, who wins in a tie?
- Identify when the Protector's powers come into effect. For example, while a Trust is revocable or amendable, the Protector's actions may be subject to the Grantor's powers to change things. As noted, with such a Trust, the Protector's powers will typically not come into play until the Trust is irrevocable at the Grantor's passing or incapacity. Once a Trust is no longer amendable, the Protector provisions are particularly important so that the Trust can adapt to changing laws or circumstances.
- Build succession provisions for the Protector into the Trust. Name a backup Protector or have a mechanism for a change in the Protector. For example, if the Protector is the lawyer that helped draft a Trust, provide that the Protector automatically changes if that attorney is discharged and the Grantor hires new legal counsel. Likewise, recognize the Protector's right to resign and otherwise decline to serve.
- Cause the Protector to be subject to the same standards of capacity to which a Trustee is subject, so if the Protector is incapacitated, the next one in line steps up.
- Define the standard of care by which the Protector's actions will be measured. Define whether the Protector is required to act (such a duty may work a hardship on the Protector), or simply has the discretion to act. Spell out where the line is

and what it takes for the Protector to cross the line in acting on behalf of or for the benefit of the Trust.

- If the Protector is given powers to remove bad Trustees, change beneficiaries' rights, exercise independent discretion to approve or disapprove Trustee actions, or do anything that someone might not like, give the Protector cover. If a Protector holds a bad actor accountable, limit the power of the bad actor to seek retribution or subvert the Trust by doing an end run around the Protector.

HISTORY OF TRUST PROTECTORS

Trust Protectors, or the equivalent functionality, are as old as Trusts themselves. The Grantor's power to appoint a Protector, like other powers, arises under common law and is tied to the ability of a person to decide what will or will not happen with their property. That power is not dependent upon statutory permission or recognition. Recently, the role of a Protector has been recognized by statute under the Uniform Trust Code. Before statutory recognition, more than one attorney told me that Trust Protectors were prohibited. Such assertions are, and were, merely an expression of ignorance.

Trust Protectors were used with offshore Trusts long before they were domesticated in the U.S., not because they were new, but because the offshore attorneys knew more about what they were doing than some domestic attorneys. The use of a Trust Protector was imported to onshore planning by the early 1990s.

Around that time, I had an argument with an attorney who claimed that using a Trust Protector was unethical. I was acting as a Trust Protector to fix a problem in a Trust. That attorney was representing one of the parties harmed by the problem, and who would benefit from my action as Protector. He kept saying throughout the process that what I was doing would not work, while at the same time demanding that I do something to resolve his client's problems.

Regardless of the attorney's protestations, as Trust Protector, I was able to fix the problem. Roughly a year later, that same attorney was giving public seminars on the virtues of using a Trust Protector. At least that demonstrates that even arrogant attorneys have the ability to learn and to change tactics when it benefits their clients, and that just because they advocate for a position when it serves their interest does not mean they actually believe it.

Statutory recognition has made it more convenient to work with attorneys who mistakenly believe that if statutes don't expressly permit something, it can't be done. However, because Trusts and Trust Protectors arise by private contract, they do not require authorization or permission from any governmental authority to exist.

While there is a place for appropriate judicial intervention, there are many circumstances in which private solutions get the same results without the cost, time delay, adversarial procedural rules, or public airing of private matters that occur in court. Drafting a Trust to avoid the necessity of going to court is a good place to start and serves the client better.

For example, not too long ago, families remained in one location, generation after generation. The son worked at the factory where Dad worked and where Granddad had worked. They all went to the same church, bought groceries at the same grocery stores, and played in the same city park year after year. Again, in today's world, it is rare for generations to stay in one place for long. We are a highly mobile society. Moving from one side of the nation to the other for new and better opportunities is easy compared to just a generation or two ago. How likely is it that your descendants will live in the same state where you form your Trust? Ultimately, the Trust will need to move with the movers. In some instances, it will move by operation of law whether or not the Trust instrument provides for it. When a Trust has no provision governing how and when its situs will change, the parties are either required to go to court or to rely on the operation of laws over which they have no control. This can force the Trust into a place where its material purposes are frustrated or subverted.

It makes far more sense to either give the power to change or determine the situs of a Trust to a Trustee or, in situations where that may not be appropriate, to a Trust Protector. This makes it possible to change the situs of the Trust to reflect the practical reality of its parties or properties with an inexpensive private action rather than a costly public proceeding in court.

TAKE THE PROTECTOR SERIOUSLY

Those unfamiliar with a Trust Protector might think they can get away with ignoring the Protector's powers. A recent case in Florida illustrates this point. In Minassian v. Rachins, 152 So.3d 719, 2014 WL 6775269 (Fla. 4th DCA December 03, 2014), a dispute arose about certain terms of a Trust. In the middle of the litigation, the Trustee appointed a Trust Protector pursuant to the terms of the Trust. The Trust Protector had the power to modify the Trust, including the power to interpret any ambiguous provision of the Trust. The trial court disallowed the Trust Protector's action. The trial court's action was reversed on appeal, and the Trust Protector's action was upheld.

I have witnessed other attorneys tell their clients they can safely violate the terms of a Trust because the Trust Protector's powers to hold them accountable don't work. Such attorneys and their clients have been sadly disappointed.

If a Trust is small and simple and immediately distributes everything after death, a Protector may be overkill. For just about every other situation, a Trust Protector is vital to the long-term operation and administration of the Trust. The absence of Protector provisions indicates that the Trust is probably missing other key provisions as well. This is particularly true of Trusts that claim to be multi-generational.

The Protector serves as a check and a balance.

DOES IT MATTER?

- If your Trust does not have a Protector, have it reviewed by an attorney who routinely implements Protector provisions. Even if a Trust has a Protector, have it reviewed and updated if it is more than a decade old. The law has evolved substantially in this area and continues to change.
- If you have an irrevocable Trust that would benefit from but does not have a Trust Protector, do not despair. There are remedies that a qualified attorney can help you implement.
- Who in your current plan serves as the check-and-balance on your Trustee? If no one, what would happen if your Trustee made decisions that conflicted with your intent?
- List the three things most likely to change about your family, your assets, or the law over the next 30 years. Does your Trust have the built-in flexibility to adapt to those changes without going to court?

This critical safeguard of the Protector keeps the system on track. Next we explore how to infuse lasting meaning into the wealth through Statements of Wishes.

CHAPTER 8

GIVING WEALTH MEANING – WISHES, VALUES AND PROTECTION

INTEGRATING VALUES

Part of the quest to formulate a Dynasty Trust that is going to outlive us is to transcend the technical and functional elements and express value, meaning, and purpose. One of the tools that can and should be built into a Trust for this very purpose is what we call Statements of Wishes. Other terms that mean essentially the same thing are an "Ethical Will" (Hebrew: "Zava'ah") or "Spiritual Will." Sometimes what are referred to as Statements of Wishes in this book take the form of a family constitution, mission statement, vision or theme.

Statements of Wishes give the Grantor and others an opportunity to memorialize what is deepest and most important in life. It is analogous to a private and personalized family sacred book, holy writing or scripture. Such expressions of value and purpose can shape the direction a Trust takes in ways that cold, clinical legal language cannot.

Statements of Wishes are non-binding precatory instructions to the Trustee and Beneficiaries. They are just "wishes" and not commandments. They permit the Grantor to make value, policy, and incentive statements that guide the Trustee on when, where, and how to exercise discretion in the administration of the Trust. They can also provide Beneficiaries with direction and information concerning what is expected of them with the benefits they receive from the Trust. Statements of Wishes help successive generations know the answer to the big question of "why?" They can and should tell a story that inspires, as we saw with Carmen and her family.

In many ways, the Statements of Wishes address the big purposes underpinning a Trust. They may be the most important element of anyone's estate plan. Avoiding probate, minimizing taxes, and protecting assets are important, but not the most important. Statements of Wishes are where you spell out what you want your estate to do for the Beneficiaries of your Trust, as opposed to what money might do for them.

Many studies indicate that some of the biggest points of frustration and conflict in successive generations arise over their predecessors' estates because they do not know why things were done the way they were or what is expected of them. When used appropriately, Statements of Wishes can remedy that deficiency that seems so pervasive in traditional estate plans.

Wealth without purpose is meaningless and destructive. Listing out your wishes attaches meaning to the money you leave behind. The greater the meaning attached to wealth, the greater the good it will accomplish in the lives of those who are touched by it. We are but temporary custodians of this world's goods. We will all depart from this mortality, but the legacy of our stewardship will outlive us and affect generations to come. Your Statements of Wishes can incentivize your Beneficiaries to enhance their life and lifestyle and improve themselves personally.

Wealth without meaning is a destructive force.

Wealth with meaning is a creative force.

When a Trust recognizes the Grantor's Statements of Wishes, it empowers the Grantor to customize the Trust to fit the unique family needs without incurring substantial attorneys' fees and without "hardwiring" in provisions that must be removed by amendment when circumstances change. Recognized statements of wishes make family values and the Grantor's wishes part of the legacy of a Trust.

As we hope is clear in reading this book, a well-drafted Trust will not merely give a Beneficiary "something for nothing." Rather, it will incorporate the Grantor's values, policy concerns, and incentives for the purpose of inspiring the Beneficiary to do what is right. Statements of Wishes are a powerful device to help maximize the long-term benefits of a Trust.

THE MEANING

Assets by themselves are neither good nor bad. Whether the outcome of giving those assets to future generations is good or bad is largely up to the Grantor. As the Grantor, you have the power to turn a potentially destructive gift of assets into a creative force for good. The outcome of such gifts is up to you more than may be obvious on the surface.

It is important to realize that how and with what meaning wealth is transferred to the next generation is probably more important than what or how substantial or small that wealth may be. Particularly in multi-generational Trusts, it is important to recognize that generational wealth transitions are going to take place repeatedly. As a result, it deepens and strengthens the power of wealth on a deep emotional level when each generation offers up their own Statements of Wishes. For that reason, better-crafted Trusts will recognize that Statements of Wishes may be made by any Grantor or any Beneficiary of the Trust and considered by the Trustee.

All parties to the Trust may be invited to consider carefully the consequences of the Trust over time and over multiple generations. Taking this task seriously will result in far greater benefits to future participants in the Trust than any measure of economic wealth.

Statements of Wishes may address a wide variety of topics and functions. For example, there may be a policy statement such as "I have always found it beneficial (or harmful) to invest in _________." Such statements do not tie the Trustee's hands but give the Trustee sound guidance in formulating an investment policy.

Likewise, Statements of Wishes may also serve as a value statement, such as "Education is important." And such a value statement can be turned into an incentive statement by saying, "Because education is important to me if a Beneficiary graduates from university, the Trustee may send them to a vacation destination of their choice (or buy them a car or give them a downpayment on the house, and so on)." When the parties to a Trust consider that the planning is more about the people than the money, they may come up with Statements of Wishes that express what matters most in terms far beyond mere policy, values, or incentives.

USE YOUR OWN WORDS

For some reason, non-lawyers believe that any legal statement they create has to "sound" like a lawyer drafted it. They cling to "lawyerese" language as if it makes the document more "real." For a number of reasons, nothing could be further from the truth.

One: Legal language is loaded with terms of art that are very crisp and specific and carry lots of baggage well beyond what the untrained mind may imagine. While it is not necessary to avoid words that may have specific legal meanings, it is also not necessary to use such words. The best words to use are those that make sense to you. Using words and phrases you understand and recognize is the surest path to communicating what you really mean.

Two: Words from the heart are powerful emotional statements. Descendants and Beneficiaries will treasure your personal words and language more than whatever wealth you may provide for them. That's especially true when your expressions are framed in words that come from the heart of someone they knew and loved.

Wealth without meaning is a destructive force.
Wealth with meaning is a creative force.

DISCRETIONARY DISTRIBUTIONS: EMPOWERING TRUSTEES WITH GUIDED JUDGMENT

Discretionary distributions are a cornerstone of effective dynasty trusts. Such provisions give Trustees the flexibility to release funds based on current needs rather than rigid rules. This approach not only adapts to life's unpredictabilities but also shields assets from external threats. By granting Trustees broad authority to make or not make distributions "as they deem advisable," a Trust can protect Beneficiaries from their own poor decisions or from creditors seeking to seize assets. Research from estate law sources emphasizes that this discretion acts as a legal barrier: creditors cannot force distributions because Beneficiaries cannot compel distributions and have no enforceable right to Trust assets until the Trustee determines it is advisable.

Such discretion of the Trustee is rarely absolute. For certain tax purposes it must be reasonably measurable and ascertainable, which typically means distributions are limited to or for the purpose of a Beneficiary's health, education, maintenance, and support (HEMS). The scope of discretion (the amount permitted to be distributed) can also be limited in some fashion, such as income only, or a specific percentage or dollar amount, a fraction of income, or a combination of such limitations such as a fraction of income with an annual dollar cap. Generally, the idea is to allow the Trustee to distribute enough but not too much to each Beneficiary. Where do draw the line between enough and too much varies significantly from family to family.

Statements of Wishes play a pivotal role here, transforming raw discretion into purposeful action. Your wishes can provide non-binding criteria for Trustees, such as prioritizing distributions for education, health, or entrepreneurial ventures that align with family values like self-reliance or community service. For instance, if a Beneficiary faces financial hardship, the Trustee might reference your wish for "responsible stewardship" to approve support only if it promotes long-term stability, rather than enabling short-term spending. Such guided discretion helps ensure your wealth fosters growth, not dependency, while maintaining the Trust's spendthrift protections, clauses that prevent Beneficiaries from assigning their interests or creditors from attaching them before distribution.

When tied to your Statements of Wishes, discretionary distributions become a dynamic tool: they protect the principal from dissipation or claims, encourage positive behaviors, and honor your legacy by making Trustees stewards of your moral compass.

BENEFICIAL ENJOYMENT WITHOUT OWNERSHIP: REAPING REWARDS WITHOUT THE RISKS

One of the most elegant features of a well-designed Trust is allowing Beneficiaries to enjoy assets without holding legal title, a concept rooted in property law that separates "equitable" (beneficial) interests from "legal" ownership. This means a Beneficiary can live in a Trust-owned home, drive a Trust-owned vehicle, or vacation at a Trust-owned property, all while the Trust retains formal ownership. Legal precedents, such as U.S. tax code Section 674 and various state statutes, confirm that this setup provides robust protection: since the Beneficiary doesn't own the asset, creditors, divorcing spouses, or lawsuits cannot easily seize it.

This structure dovetails perfectly with Statements of Wishes, enabling you to define how enjoyment aligns with family principles. For example, your wishes might specify that an heirloom property such as a family cabin is for "gathering generations to build bonds and create memories," guiding Trustees to maintain it for joint family use rather than selling it for quick cash. Or, for a business interest, you could spell out your desire that Beneficiaries "participate in operations to learn stewardship," allowing them managerial roles without ownership vulnerability. Research from Trust law resources highlights that this "beneficial enjoyment" not only minimizes tax exposure (e.g., no capital gains on Trust-held appreciating assets) but also discourages reckless behavior. Beneficiaries know they can't borrow against or sell what they don't own.

By incorporating beneficial enjoyment provisions along with spend thrift provisions, informed by your Statements of Wishes, the Trust becomes a shield: it delivers the joys of wealth without exposing it to the perils of direct ownership, ensuring your legacy endures through protected, purposeful use.

LOANS OVER OUTRIGHT DISTRIBUTIONS: FOSTERING ACCOUNTABILITY AND GROWTH

In Dynasty Trusts, shifting from outright distributions to loans can transform inheritance from a potential curse into a catalyst for self-reliance. Instead of gifting funds, the Trust acts as a "family bank," lending money with terms like interest rates, repayment schedules, and collateral requirements. Estate planning studies show this preserves principal (loans return to the Trust) while teaching financial responsibility. Beneficiaries must demonstrate viable plans, such as starting a business or buying a home, to secure funding. This mirrors venture capital models, where "skin in the game" motivates success and reduces waste.

This can be linked to Statements of Wishes by outline loan guidelines. For instance, you can spell out that loans should only be made to support "ventures that build character and independence," prioritizing educational pursuits or ethical businesses over luxury spending. If a Beneficiary proposes a startup, Trustees could reference your wish for "productive innovation" to approve a low-interest loan secured by future earnings. Unlike mandatory distributions (which can trigger immediate taxes or creditor exposure), loans defer tax events and enhance spendthrift protections because creditors can't claim secured loaned funds as easily as funds that have been distributed.

This approach, drawn from advanced Trust strategies, not only grows the Trust's assets through interest but also instills values: Beneficiaries learn to earn, repay, and create, turning your wealth into a legacy of empowered producers rather than passive consumers.

AVOID THE MANDATORY DISTRIBUTION TRAP: A CAUTIONARY TALE

Mandatory distributions, requiring Trustees to release funds at set ages or milestones, or permitted Beneficiaries to compel such distributions, can undermine even the strongest spendthrift safeguards, exposing wealth to immediate risks.

Consider what happened to Jack, a young entrepreneur whose parents' Trust mandated full principal payout at age 45. Jack was mostly successful as a business owner, but suffered a big setback just after the passing of his parents. Because Jack was then 48 years old, and the distribution was automatic and mandatory based on his age, his creditors asked the court to compel the Trust to distribute the assets. This bypassed the Trust's creditor protections, and Jack lost his entire inheritance. What began as a well-intentioned "maturity milestone" became a financial disaster, leaving Jack without an inheritance and the total loss of family generational wealth.

Research from Trust litigation cases reveals this common flaw: mandatory distributions or the power of Beneficiaries to compel distributions results in Beneficiaries being treated as owners, nullifying spendthrift clauses designed to block assignments or attachments. When distributions are discretionary, and based on Statements of Wishes, this outcome is avoided. Statements of Wishes in combination with other protections under a Trust can provide flexible, need-based access guided by values like "prudent stewardship," empowering Trustees to delay or condition payouts. For example, your Statements of Wishes may give the Trustees guidance to base distributions on an evaluation of "financial maturity" and the absence of risk factors that would compromise or destroy the family wealth.

By steering clear of rigid mandates and leveraging wishes for guided discretion, your Trust becomes resilient: it protects against life's pitfalls, honors your vision, and ensures wealth serves rather than sabotages future generations.

KEEPING WEALTH INSIDE THE TRUST: THE TRUE ENGINE OF MULTI-GENERATIONAL STRENGTH

Every tool we've explored in this chapter: statements of wishes, discretionary distributions, beneficial enjoyment without ownership, loans instead of gifts, and avoiding mandatory age-based payouts, serves one overarching purpose: keeping the assets inside the Trust for as long as possible. When wealth leaves the Trust and becomes property of the Beneficiaries, the protections collapse. Spendthrift clauses no longer shield against creditors, divorce claims, or poor decisions. The Beneficiary becomes the outright owner, and the wealth is suddenly vulnerable to every risk the Trust was designed to block. When wealth leaves the Trust, all of the Trust benefits collapse.

The opposite approach, retaining assets inside a properly structured Dynasty Trust, creates a fortress that protects and compounds wealth across generations. Because the Beneficiary never receives legal title, creditors generally cannot reach Trust-owned assets, and the spendthrift protections hold firm. Beneficial enjoyment lets family members live well (homes, education, business opportunities) without the dangers of ownership. Loans foster accountability and return capital to the Trust for future use. Discretionary distributions guided by your Statements of Wishes ensure money flows only for purposes that align with your values, education, entrepreneurship, family unity, charitable impact, rather than impulse or entitlement.

This is the fullest and best implementation of the old adage, "own nothing but control everything."

One of the most powerful financial advantages emerges when the Trust is GST-exempt (Generation-Skipping Transfer Tax exclusion allocated at creation). Assets owned by the Trust are not included in the taxable estate of any Beneficiary. This single feature eliminates estate tax at every generation, allowing wealth to compound tax-free indefinitely.

THE DYNASTY CONTRAST

Consider the dramatic difference across four generations of traditional approaches and the Dynasty Trust approach:

Traditional Approach: Outright Transfers with Estate Tax

Genera-tion	Starting Value	After Growth (30 yrs)	Estate-Tax (40%)	Net Inheritance
You (G1)	$30,000,000	$172,443,520	$68,977,408	$103,466,112
Children (G2)	$103,466,112	$594,204,313	$237,681,725	$356,522,588
Grand children (G3)	$356,522,588	$2,047,291,966	$818,916,786	$1,228,375,180
Great-Grand children (G4)	$1,228,375,180	$7,053,597,876	—	$7,053,597,876

Total estate taxes paid across three generations: $1,125,575,919

That's over $1.1 billion lost to taxes, money that could have remained in your family.

Dynasty Trust Approach: GST-Exempt Structure

Generation	Trust Value	After Growth (30 yrs)	Transfer Tax	Available to Family
You (G1)	$30,000,000	$172,443,520	$0	$172,443,520
Children (G2)	$172,443,520	$990,254,476	$0	$990,254,476
Grand children (G3)	$990,254,476	$5,686,803,790	$0	$5,686,803,790
Great-Grand-children (G4)	$5,686,803,790	$32,654,018,894	$0	$32,654,018,894

Total transfer taxes paid: $0

The difference is staggering: one path hemorrhages over a billion dollars to taxes and risks; the other preserves and multiplies it tax-free, generation after generation.

It is a giant mistake to conclude that this only works for families with tens of millions of dollars. Families that implemented this planning a hundred years ago with less than a million dollars today enjoy enormous wealth. True dynasty planning is not about where you are starting from, but where you are going.

Your Statements of Wishes are the compass that keeps this engine running true. They guide Trustees to favor retention over distribution, to prioritize loans that build character and businesses, to allow beneficial enjoyment that strengthens family bonds, and to exercise discretion in ways that honor your deepest values: self-reliance, stewardship, generosity, and legacy. When assets stay inside the Trust, protected by your wishes and the law's most powerful tools, wealth becomes more than money: it becomes a force for enduring family strength, purpose, and impact.

The choice is yours. You can hand off assets and watch them erode through taxes, claims, and poor decisions, or you can build a Trust that keeps the wealth working, growing, and protected for centuries.

The only wealth that has the potential to have meaning, is the wealth that we possess. In this chapter we have seen how Statements of Wishes, discretionary distributions, beneficial enjoyment, loans, and avoiding mandatory traps keep assets working inside the Trust: protected, growing, and purposeful. These are not one-time fixes; they are moves in the infinite game of Dynasty planning. Unlike the finite game of conventional estate planning (divide the assets, pay the taxes, hope for the best), the infinite game never ends. Every decision, whether to distribute now or retain for later, whether to give outright or lend with purpose, shapes not just the next generation's starting point, but the family's capacity to keep playing, adapting, and winning together for centuries. Your Statements of Wishes and the related tools are the playbook that keeps the game noble and the players strong.

That is the real power of giving wealth meaning.

DOES IT MATTER?

- Does your Trust expressly acknowledge and recognize that you may make Statements of Wishes and authorize the Trustees to rely on your wishes in the exercise of discretion? If not, why not, and do you care? You may wish to make sure your Trust accommodates your Statements of Wishes.
- Ask yourself if it is important to you to let your descendants know what you have done and what you expect of them. What part of who you are do you want to be remembered and enrich your family from generation to generation?

- Whether your Trust expressly calls for or permits reliance on your Statements of Wishes, I strongly encourage you to write your wishes down in any event. What advice do you have for those who will travel the path after you? Share it. The future will appreciate it more than anything else you leave behind.
- As you put your Statements of Wishes into words, note why you have that particular wish. For example, you may indicate that you have a particular wish because it "demonstrates high moral standards," will "build confidence," or will "contribute to long-term health," or "I wish I had done that when I was younger," and so forth. The "why" is a big part of what gives your Statements of Wishes so much power in influencing future generations for good because the advice or wishes come straight from the heart.
- You may want to put your Statements of Wishes in the form of a letter to future generations that shares your philosophies, experiences, lessons learned, joys, and personal values. View it as your "last shot" at direct communication with your loved ones and descendants. This is the part of your estate plan that they will remember and rely on the most. It's important to consider what your so-called last words should be and the emotional impact those words will have on the people who come after you.
- Have you considered whether your current Trust (or planned Trust) allows assets to stay inside the Trust for multiple generations, or whether mandatory distributions force them out at set ages, creating windows where creditors, lawsuits, or poor decisions can drain them?
- Does your plan include discretionary distributions guided by your Statements of Wishes, so Trustees can say "no" to requests that don't align with your values (education,

entrepreneurship, family unity) while still protecting the principal?

- Are Beneficiaries allowed beneficial enjoyment of Trust assets (homes, education, business opportunities) without ever receiving legal title, preserving spendthrift protections and shielding wealth from creditors or divorce claims?
- Have you structured the Trust to favor loans over outright distributions? What guidelines in your Statements of Wishes could encourage responsible borrowing and repayment, turning inheritance into a tool for building rather than consuming?

With meaning and values now embedded in the plan, next we look to the future: capturing social capital and preparing the next generation without surprise.

CHAPTER 9

TRUST THE FUTURE – CAPTURING SOCIAL CAPITAL AND BEYOND

CAPTURE SOCIAL CAPITAL

A certain amount of all wealth is going to be confiscated by politicians. It is as inevitable as the proverbial "death and taxes." This confiscation takes at least two forms: Taxes and inflation. Ironically, inflationary policies are tax hikes in disguise. Inflation is taxed both as capital gains and as estate taxes. Inflation also pushes taxpayers into higher brackets for income tax purposes. Any long-term plan must consider that inflation and taxation are going to happen. Even if a part of the wealth is going to be grabbed in any event, there are ways to minimize how much ends up in the hands of the politicians.

There are several methods by which well-structured Trusts and other devices can mitigate the various taxes on inflation disguised as appreciation. The capital gains tax can be reduced or eliminated with a step-up in cost basis if the asset is included in your taxable estate, typically in a revocable Trust. The Estate taxes on inflation can be avoided if the asset is NOT included in your taxable estate, typically in an irrevocable Trust. In any event, whether the asset is or is not included in your taxable estate, Capital Gains taxes can be reduced through a variety of exemptions and deferred through a number of mechanisms, most notably tax-free exchanges.

When such options are exhausted, and either the capital gains taxes or the estate taxes are inevitable, it is possible to harvest wealth that would be otherwise lost to such taxes in certain tax-exempt charitable structures. A powerful tool that I strongly recommend you explore for charitable giving is a Donor Advised Fund (DAF). You can learn more about DAFs by reaching out to Legacy Global Foundation at www.LegacyGlobal.org or 1+602.704.1000. They are an independent organization not tied to any particular financial platform, geography, or cause. Part of what makes them unique is their willingness to accept gifts of alternative non-cash assets, their willingness to work with your financial advisor, and their capacity to arrange charitable giving anywhere in the world.

On the one hand, such wealth is no longer "yours" or your family's per se. You can't use it for your lifestyle or give it to your children. You can, however, participate in the decision-making process on how and for what purposes it is used to help others. Once rescued from taxation, this so-called "social capital" can then be available for your family to use in causes you support. You can either send the money off to the politicians through taxation and let them decide how it is spent, or it can go to charities and social causes that you choose. Who do you trust more to make good decisions with your money, yourself or the politicians? It is that simple.

You can throw more of your hard-earned money into the political pit and the private scams, or you can give it to charities you have vetted and/or spend it on social causes that you carefully choose. There is a reason that the richest people in the world often end up with charities named after them.

IT REALLY IS YOUR CHOICE.

Another often-overlooked fact of the real world is that giving money to charity expands wealth. Some people falsely believe that one must have wealth before giving is even possible. In fact, charitable giving triggers the creation of wealth.

I have worked with a number of families who started with nothing and, while living on a small fraction of their income, either reinvested or gave the rest to charity. I have watched as they amassed enormous fortunes while being profoundly generous. More often than not, this pattern is not new but has been developed and refined in the family over many generations. I have seen that when charitable giving is a part of the family culture, generation after generation continues to live on a fraction of what they make and structure their business deals so that wealth flows back to the family group and otherwise supports vigorous and deliberate charitable giving. Such families are not just rich; they have actual multi-generational wealth. In my perception, charitable giving is the beginning and source of such wealth, not the result of it.

Even when he was a child and even as a poor adult, the amazingly wealthy John D. Rockefeller always gave what he could to people in need. Long before he donated millions to worthy causes, he donated nickels and dimes to people in need. His personal giving was based on a policy adopted early in life, quite apart from the amount of wealth he gained later in life.

People who give create more wealth. Suppose you examine the lives of two people starting at equal positions, both with nothing. In that case, only one gives to charity, and the other does not. Over time, the one who gives to charity will have a far greater probability of becoming wealthy.

Integrated planning and a well-formed Trust will incorporate charitable structures that both mitigate taxes and preserve the family's control or influence over social capital and, at the same time, place your family in a position to further increase the store of "seed corn" for the benefit of future generations.

CHARITABLE PLANNING AS TRAINING FOR THE NEXT GENERATION

Charitable planning is more than a tax strategy; it is a profound tool for preparing the next generation to steward wealth responsibly. By integrating family foundations or Donor Advised Funds (DAFs) into your Dynasty Trust, you create a hands-on classroom where heirs learn discernment, empathy, and long-term impact. Imagine your children or grandchildren participating in grant-making decisions, evaluating proposals, visiting causes, and measuring outcomes. This shifts their view from wealth as personal entitlement to a shared resource for good, fostering skills in analysis, collaboration, and ethical judgment that translate to business and family governance.

Family foundations, in particular, can serve as a "mini board" experience, where younger members rotate roles in reviewing applications or site visits, guided by your Statements of Wishes. This not only captures social capital (redirecting what would be lost to taxes) but also instills a culture of generosity that combats the entitlement pitfalls of unearned wealth.

As Johann Kurtz articulates in his book *Leaving a Legacy: Inheritance, Charity, & Thousand-Year Families*, "True charity is a multi-generational project—and virtuous family dynasties are its indispensable guardians." Kurtz emphasizes that blending inheritance with structured philanthropy builds resilient families, turning potential consumers into stewards who sustain prosperity for centuries. By involving the next generation early, your charitable structures become a bridge to self-reliance, equipping them to lead with purpose.

THE PROSPERITY PERSPECTIVE: INVESTING IN PEOPLE FOR HOLISTIC THRIVING

Dynasty planning's true power lies not just in amassing financial assets, but in building resilient people who thrive on every level, economically, emotionally, socially, and spiritually. If all we do is make a lot of money and ruin the people in the process, we just continue to feed the wealth destruction cycle. The mechanism for breaking the negative cycle and initiating a healthy positive wealth cycle is to invest in the people.

For there to be multi-generational wealth, there must be a continuing cycle of new generations. This means the family is not an afterthought or a luxury to be acquired once it is affordable. Getting married and having children is not only central, it is the source of wealth building capacity and enjoyment.

When families shift from viewing wealth as mere money to a tool for family and personal development, the consequences ripple across generations in profound ways. Research on multi-generational families shows that those who prioritize "human capital" don't just preserve wealth; they multiply it as part of the process of creating stronger, more unified family bonds.

This perspective starts with recognizing that economic prosperity alone can hollow out families, breeding entitlement and isolation. But when the wealth creation process is not relegated to the bread winner, but an enterprise for the whole family, integrated with tools like family councils, Statements of Wishes, and focused time together, such investments yield returns of long-lasting high-quality family members and relationships. The ongoing financial prosperity becomes a byproduct of a healthy resilient family.

When the family estate and business enterprises are used by older generations to personally teach and model self-reliance, lifetime learning, hard work, collaboration, conflict resolution and productivity, a completely different relationship with the financial wealth emerges. Intentional family councils turn mere discussions into training grounds: next generations learn governance through shared decisions, fostering emotional intelligence and a capacity for long-term prosperity that no bank account can buy.

Families that invest in people report higher life satisfaction, lower conflict rates, and greater resilience to setbacks. Studies of enduring dynasties reveal that such families excel not just financially, but in mental health, community impact, and intergenerational harmony. Marriage and children expand the talent pool. Divorce rates decline, and when it happens a vigorous support network and keeping the money in the family makes recovery faster.

By weaving the Dynasty Trust and planning tools discussed in this book with deliberate investments of time and training in the family, a healthy muti-generational wealth cycle is initiated and perpetuated that will thrive and prosper far into the future.

If you are reading this and having a sense that your family is so broken or dysfunctional that it cannot measure up to this standard, the intended message is getting lost in translation. All families have challenges, even the most successful. The point is that wherever your family is at now, the intention and investment in implementing and applying multi-generational dynastic planning will change the trajectory of your family and it will produce vastly improved results both financially and in the how the people turn out.

RESILIENT DYNASTIES: THE WEALTH MENTALITY ADVANTAGE

One of most overlooked consequences of such family integrated Dynasty planning is forging a "wealth mentality" or "prosperity perspective". This is a resilient mindset that enables families to thrive in every aspect of life, and perhaps most importantly to recover from catastrophic losses and emerge stronger. History shows that families with this mentality don't just survive economic disasters; they regenerate wealth because they know how to create it anew.

One example is elite Chinese lineages that rebounded after communist revolutions stripped them of everything: despite total confiscation of material wealth and social status, over time descendants regained what was taken from them through transmitted values like work ethic, social networks, and independent learning. In every case, regenerating lost wealth happened when parents directly took responsibility for training children rather than relegating it to the state or third parties. When that direct parent child connection was disrupted, no such recovery occurred. Such resilience stems from viewing people as the most important resource which makes wealth acquisition a renewable skill, not a finite trophy.

In your Dynasty plan, this mentality is cultivated deliberately by spending time with family members. Planning tools like Statements of Wishes function best when they are communicated personally. That is the reason for emphasizing family councils. It is in the context of personal interaction that such tools help articulate and instill a family ethos of stewardship and innovation. "We build, not consume; we recover through unity; there is no challenge we cannot overcome together."

Family councils reinforce such a wealth culture through real-world training: simulating loss scenarios or debating recoveries builds emotional fortitude. Spiritual and cultural traditions are woven into the fabric of the family's relationships and activities. Economic volatility and social turmoil are seen as opportunities for innovation, not threats. Family members not only learn to read and interpret financial statements and business plans, they learn to read and understand people, society, and the flow of organizations. They learn to discern right from wrong, and what is real from what is illusory. The legal structures of Dynasty Planning provide integrated tools, but it is in the family that people learn what they are and how to use them and what they mean.

The payoff is significant. Families that do what it takes to foster this mind set weather divorces, bankruptcies, health care crisis, and economic crashes without total collapse. Research on multi-generational wealth persistence shows that such Dynasties recover 2-3 times faster than average, often exceeding prior peaks because they've honed skills in human capital and opportunity spotting. Unlike fragile fortunes built on luck or the popularity of fleeting fades, your Dynasty, when rooted in people, correct values, reality, and adaptable structures, will become antifragile: not just surviving loss, but thriving because of it.

This is the ultimate family consequence: generations equipped to turn setbacks into comebacks, ensuring prosperity endures no matter what forces array against it.

Families with a wealth mentality don't just inherit prosperity. They recreate it, turning every loss into a lesson for greater gains.

INHERITANCE VS. CHARITY: THE VIRTUOUS BALANCE

A common dilemma arises: Should you leave an inheritance to your descendants, risking entitlement and depletion, or give everything to charity, forcing them to build from scratch? The extreme of full disinheritance, channeling all wealth to causes outside the family, may seem noble, but it often backfires. Without a foundation, the next generation may lack the capital, networks, or training to thrive, perpetuating cycles of struggle rather than prosperity. Kurtz warns against this in *Leaving a Legacy*, noting that modern philanthropy often prioritizes short-term "impact" over enduring family duty, fracturing legacies that could amplify good across eras.

The better path is balance: Provide inheritance not as handouts, but as tools: access to capital via Family Bank loans, business opportunities through Trust-owned entities, and life training via family councils and charitable involvement. This empowers heirs to create their own wealth while honoring your values.

Unlike outright charity giveaways, it builds capacity: your Statements of Wishes can condition support on milestones like education or ethical ventures, turning potential "trust-fund babies" into producers. Research on multi-generational families shows this hybrid approach yields stronger outcomes: wealth grows, families unite, and charity becomes a family tradition, not a one-time purge. Disinheriting robs heirs of resources; equipping them multiplies your impact, creating dynasties that sustain both private prosperity and public good.

Whether you choose to blend inheritance with charity, retain assets inside the Trust, or redirect social capital through a Family Foundation, the guiding mindset remains the same: this is an infinite game. The goal is not to "win" by handing over the largest pile at death, but to equip each generation with the tools, capital, training, and values to keep the game going, stronger, wiser, and more generous than the last. Charity becomes part of the playbook, not the end of the story. When families play for continuity rather than consumption, wealth stops being a finite resource to be divided and starts being a renewable force that builds both private prosperity and public good across eras.

ISN'T THIS GOVERNING FROM THE GRAVE?

The purpose of multi-generational Dynasty planning is self-reliance. It is not to rule from the grave or to make decisions in advance. Quite the opposite. The purpose of Dynasty planning is to give future generations the tools and the moral guidance they will need to self-govern and build their own wealth as opposed to simply consuming what they received from you.

It is a basic and universal law of money that unearned wealth is not respected. It is simply part of being human to care more about what we worked hard to create than we do about something given to us for nothing. Someone with no "skin in the game" in creating wealth doesn't have any commitment to protecting or growing that wealth. It is just a "freebee," and therefore, it has no personal value. Those who simply inherit wealth without participating in its creation don't have the investment of time, energy, sweat, heart, and soul needed to protect and grow that wealth, so they have no real investment in it. That's one of the key reasons the management of inherited wealth goes off the rails.

The irony of inherited wealth is that just giving people unrestricted and unearned purchasing power destroys their capacity to make choices and brings them into bondage. A Dynasty Trust expands choices, but it does not take them away.

In the end, who has more choices: The one who is able to consume the principal down to zero through bad choices and riotous living, or the one who has multi-generational access to a growing pool of capital that they are able to deploy through their own efforts to create greater wealth?

Who has more freedom, the one who is dependent upon wealth created by past generations, or the one with the capacity to create new wealth of their own?

Transferring wealth through an Integrated Dynasty Trust does more than just preserve wealth for the use and enjoyment of future generations. It makes it possible for them to generate wealth of their own. It also helps protect the people and perpetuate the family.

DO NOT SURPRISE THEM WHEN YOU'RE DEAD

As we near the end of this journey, one critical topic remains: how to discuss money, estates, businesses, and Trusts with your children and grandchildren. Consider the topic of sex. Most people probably consider this topic more than they would care to admit. Consider it in the context of what kind of conversations we should have about sex with children.

Waiting until they're teenagers, in college, or facing relationship struggles is too late. "The talk" must happen much sooner. Ideally, children witness a healthy, loving relationship modeled by their parents and learn early, from their family, at age-appropriate times, that sex can be joyful and fulfilling in the right context, or destructive and dangerous in the wrong one. Timing and circumstances determine its lifelong impact.

Now, apply this to money. Avoiding conversations about wealth and inheritance isn't the answer. While some details aren't their business, our inevitable passing means that it will be their concern eventually. Surprising heirs or Beneficiaries with unexpected wealth usually backfires. Even without the troubles seen in cases like Jack and Kim, Beneficiaries are rarely ready for a sudden windfall. "Windfall psychology" mirrors the lottery's effects, including the emotional, spiritual, and social fallout. People tend to overspend or mismanage unearned wealth, thwarting the intentions of those who produced it. There's a gap between getting what you want and wanting what you get, and unearned wealth exacts hidden costs.

Preparation changes this. When people see it coming, they have time to prepare emotionally and spiritually for the money before it arrives. They can spend it in their mind many times over and think through what they really want to do before they can spend it in fact. If the next generation knows that they are not just going to get the money, that it is going to be in a Trust, that the amount they get will be capped, that they will need to work to feed themselves, that how much they get, if any, will depend in part on how productive they are, then the next generation tends to handle their inheritance in a much more effective and healthy way.

Alternatively, if the message you broadcast to the next generation is that you're too stupid to understand money, that you are too lazy to make money, that we can't talk about money, and that in spite of all that I'm just going to give you all my money anyway and when I'm dead you can do as you please without consequences, then the next generation can't wait for their parents to die. They resent how their parents' money takes away their incentives to be useful humans. And when their parents finally pass, they fall off the deep end financially and with everything that matters most. The messages we send the next generation about money help determine how fast the generational wealth cycle wheel turns.

Incidentally, asking your children their opinion on what you should do with your estate can backfire. The least prepared family members are most likely to tell you to just shut up and give them the money. They think they know what to do with it. They believe they don't need any restrictions or protection from you. They will have their own plans. They know they are perfectly capable of handling it without any safety net. This is just human nature. Everyone wants money. But that very nature can make us unqualified to render an opinion as to the best way to get something for nothing. Giving children of any age what they want may not be best. Of all people involved in the generational wealth cycle, the next generation can be the least qualified to know what they should want. Those in the next generation who are prepared, integrated into the family operations, and invested in the future of the family will recognize the value of the asset protection, tax benefits, and multi-generational growth that the dynasty structure makes possible.

A Dynasty Trust expands choices, but it does not take them away.

DOES IT MATTER?

- I strongly suggest you research articles and resources about Family Councils. In such a context, here are some good ways to start a health conversation:
- Tell them your legal and financial affairs are in order and you have a plan, and they don't need to worry about it (assuming, of course, that you do).
- If you have a diagram or image illustrating your estate structures, share that with them and explain the various elements.

- Show them your Estate Planning Notebook or tell them where it is so they can find it.
- Share your Statements of Wishes with them and talk about your family's values, goals, and mission.
- Tell your children what you wish your parents had told you.
- If your children are adults, they need their own estate plans. Ask them if their affairs are in order. You may even want to assist them in obtaining whatever level of planning they need. When families are involved in multi-generational planning and business ventures, it can be beneficial if the generations coordinate with each other and use some of the same advisors.
- Introduce them to your advisory team, particularly your attorney, CPA, and financial advisors. Consider inviting one of your advisors to a family council to explain your estate plan so that the next generation has a better grasp of their roles and what to expect.
- How much daily time are you currently investing directly in your children and grandchildren (reading, conversations, shared activities) versus outsourcing childcare, tutoring, or enrichment to institutions or professionals? What small, incremental shift in your schedule could increase that personal presence and model the values you want them to carry forward?
- Does your family have regular, intentional moments (beyond holidays) where you are fully present together, without devices or distractions? Do you eat meals together? Research shows even small daily investments in family time (e.g., 20-30 minutes of focused interaction) can enhance children's emotional regulation, social skills, and long-term mental

health. How might you protect or expand those moments starting this week?

- Are family councils being used as a vehicle to give upcoming generations real leadership roles, perhaps letting teens chair a meeting, young adults lead a charitable grant decision, or next-gen members propose Family Bank investment ideas? What would happen if you assigned one upcoming family member a small leadership responsibility in the next council?
- In your family business or Trust-owned enterprises, are younger members given meaningful positions where they can gain hands-on experience, make decisions, and, importantly, learn safely from failure? How could structured roles in these enterprises build their confidence, work ethic, and wealth-creation skills while strengthening collective family resilience?
- If a major financial setback occurred tomorrow (market crash, lawsuit, business failure), would your family have the "wealth mentality" to recover and rebuild, because they've been trained to create value rather than just consume it? What one practice (e.g., family council recovery simulations, Statements of Wishes emphasizing perseverance) could you start now to cultivate that resilience?
- Get a copy of "The Ten Most Common Estate Planning Mistakes" written by David Phillips. Read it and share it with your children. You can find that book and others, and connect with David at EPMEZ.com or 480.899.1102.
- Reach out to Legacy Global Foundation at www.LegacyGlobal.org or 1+602.704.1000 and explore how you can integrate charitable giving in your dynasty plan, starting with setting up a DAF as a "family foundation"

- No matter your family's current financial position or the ages of its members, it is never too late to begin investing in people through time, values, and structured opportunities. What is one small step you can take this month to move your family toward a prosperity perspective that thrives on every level: economic, emotional, social, and spiritual?

With the future now in focus, we conclude with the vision of what is possible when it all works.

CHAPTER 10

EPILOGUE – WHEN IT WORKS, IT WORKS

THE WHEELS TURN ROUND AND ROUND

Traditional estate planning fails when it focuses solely on transferring wealth without considering the long-term impact on people. The experiences of families like Bob and Sue, Al and Liz, Carmen, Kim, and Jack illustrate a common problem: unearned wealth, without the ability or drive to create more, becomes toxic. This contributes to the universal "shirtsleeves to shirtsleeves in three generations" cycle: wealth is built, transferred, enjoyed, and then depleted. Variations of this proverb exist globally, reflecting a recurring pattern: hard work brings prosperity, which is passed to a generation that doesn't toil, leading to self-indulgence, incompetence, and eventual ruin, restarting the cycle in poverty.

Each generation views this differently. The wealth creators lament their children's lack of effort and sense of entitlement. The inheritors see no need to work amid abundance. The destroyers feel cheated and chase quick fixes or plunder. The impoverished wonder if escape is possible or worth the struggle. This cycle, earning, churning, and burning wealth, repeats endlessly, leaving each generation questioning the value of the effort.

A successful estate plan goes beyond tax or probate avoidance; it shapes family and society. Asset protection, often misunderstood, isn't just about external threats such as creditors or lawsuits, but also internal ones, like the family's own behavior. The greatest risk to wealth lies within, and true protection starts there.

This cycle mirrors timeless human archetypes: Greek fate, Hindu karma, the law of the harvest, Confucian dynasty shifts, Zen self-reflection, or the rhythmic Tao. Most live unaware of their place in it or their role in perpetuating it. Recognizing the cycle is one step; disrupting it is another. Some families have sustained wealth across generations without harming their people, proving it's possible.

The secret isn't luck. It's also more than intent. Breaking the cycle requires a deliberate, multi-generational plan, not just a short-term fix. Dynasty Planning looks beyond the present, equipping families with tools to preserve both financial and human legacies for the future.

KARMIC COMING TOGETHER

One day, after different family councils coincidentally discussed their respective parents' estates, a group of next-generation friends got together for a social event. It did not take them long to discover that they had each had a similar conversation with their parents on the very same day. It was weird. The friends talked long into the night. They were the next generation in the families of Bob and Sue, Al and Liz, Carmen, Kim, Jack, and others whose stories we have heard. They came up with a plan.

They found advisors who shared their vision for helping their families escape the wealth destruction cycle. They put together plans designed to help their next generations be strong, independent, and resilient, and to protect and grow multi-generational wealth. They formed strong social connections. Their children knew each other, played together, became friends, and grew up to become business partners and collaborators.

They each established a number of Dynasty Trusts. They set up a series of business entities owned by these Trusts. They each had a management company they called a "Family Office" to run their enterprises. They each set up partnerships among their Trusts that they called their "Family Bank" to own their various properties, investments, and enterprises. They each established a "Family Foundation" and created a family culture of using their wealth to help and serve others. They wisely employed powerful financial tools that leveraged their generational wealth.

They taught their children from a young age how to work, live modestly, and handle, manage, and grow wealth. Their children, with good training, excellent mentors, and access to capital, made their own money independent of their parents. They were able to "piggyback" with their parents' Dynasty Estate Plan and both protect and grow their wealth. They had happy marriages, raised amazing children, honored their divine heritage and eternal purposes in life, and were down-to-earth, good, honest, hardworking people. They not only lived well but also served others and contributed back to the family's wealth and to society. Their families simply thrived and prospered. I am blessed to say they have been my neighbors, clients, and friends.

THE TRAIL'S END

I love to hike a beautiful trail through the Superstition Mountains near my home. It runs in a rugged twenty-mile loop that takes you to see stunning landscapes, box canyons, whiskey-colored springs, ancient ruins, amazing rock formations, and desert wildlife only encountered far away from people. Part of the trail's beauty is that it ends where it begins.

We have walked the trail of this book with Bob and Sue, Jim, Al and Liz, Carmen, Kim, Jack, and many others. We have seen that they learned valuable lessons from the mistakes of others. Perhaps that is the true meaning of wisdom. Their children and the next generation benefit from those lessons.

I acknowledge that my wife and I have our own Dynasty Estate Plan. We do our own best to "eat our own cooking" as the saying goes. Part of that plan includes a 500-year plan for Durfee Law Group. We recruit young, smart, talented attorneys and paraprofessionals and train them in the principles, strategies, tactics, and logistics of Dynasty Estate Planning. That way, when I am no longer available or willing to show up at the office every day, highly qualified, well-trained, and very capable attorneys and others are available to assist the next generation of our clients. Perhaps I have written this book for all of those next-generation travelers.

I hope you have enjoyed the journey.

Their families simply thrived and prospered.

YOUR DYNASTY STARTS NOW

Reflect on your journey through this book. What one shift, from conventional to dynasty thinking, could transform your family's future? Use the checklists in Appendices A and B to start: Hold your first family council this month. Draft your Statements of Wishes this week. Consult an advisor aligned with these principles today. If your family is new to wealth or caught up in the wealth destruction cycle, let the negative cycle break with you. Start a new family dynasty cycle of your own. Your choices will echo for centuries one way or the other. Choose wisely. Share appropriate parts of your story with others to help them on their journey: for resources or to share your story, visit DurfeeLawGroup.com. Live well. Leave a legacy.

DOES IT MATTER?

Nothing is gained unless there is a change in a beneficial direction. As you went through this book, you had a few impressions of some things you should do. Do not waste another second. Write them down so you remember. Then do them, now if possible. Take action. Remember, children and yet-unborn generations are counting on you to make the right move.

- What legacy do you want your family to celebrate about your choices?
- What is one small, realistic step you can take today to start building that legacy?
- Share appropriate parts of your experiences with others to help them on their Journey on Amazon at https://a.co/d/0hYvSTkM or on Google at https://share.google/DFOksc0ukOEJPhXYN

SHOULD I TRUST MY TRUST?

Hopefully, this book has given you some things to consider about your Trust. If you have a Trust, read it. Take it to a qualified attorney and have it reviewed. Ask questions that matter to you.

- Is your Trust appropriate for you, your family, and your assets
- Is there anything you learned in reading this book that you want to implement in your Trust?
- Does it give your family the level of asset protection that they need or will need?

- Is it a single-use, throw-away Trust that goes away after you pass, or does it have the type of multi-generational dynasty tools you have learned about in this book?
- Have you done what you were told you should do in the letters of instruction that you received with your Trust?
- Have all your assets been transferred to your Trust?
- Is a Trust alone enough for your estate, or do you need more?
- If you have business entities, are they owned by the Trust?
- If you don't have a business, why are you paying more in taxes than you need to?
- Should you schedule a review conference with the attorney or planner who prepared your Trust?
- If a non-attorney prepared your Trust, is that sufficient? Is it what you really want?
- If you do not have a Trust, you probably need one if you're reading this book. Get on that.
- Select a qualified attorney or estate planner who is familiar with the planning issues raised in this book. Many highly qualified attorneys practice in this area, so check them out carefully.

APPENDIX A

DYNASTY TRUST CHECKLIST

QUICK-REFERENCE DYNASTY TRUST CHECKLIST

This checklist distills the core principles, tools, and questions from this book into a practical reference. Use it before you build, while you build, and long after your Trust is in place. A true Dynasty Trust is not just a document; it is a living system designed to protect people, grow wealth, and perpetuate family strength across generations.

BEFORE YOU BUILD: CORE QUESTIONS TO CLARIFY INTENT (CHAPTERS 1-3)

- Have you clearly defined what matters most to you beyond money (family harmony, self-reliance, meaningful contribution, spiritual values)?
- Do you want a single-use Trust (avoid probate/taxes only) or a multi-generational Dynasty Trust (preserve and grow people + wealth indefinitely)?
- Have you witnessed or can you imagine inherited wealth causing conflict, entitlement, overspending, or family division? What specific risks worry you most?

- Is your current (or planned) Trust funded with all major assets (real estate, business interests, retirement accounts, life insurance)?
- Does your plan protect against internal threats (addiction, divorce, poor judgment) as well as external ones (lawsuits, creditors, taxes)?
- Are you prepared to have open, age-appropriate conversations with the next generation about money, work, and legacy?

WHILE YOU BUILD: ESSENTIAL FEATURES OF A HIGH-FUNCTIONING DYNASTY TRUST (CHAPTERS 4-7)

- Is your Trust fully self-governing (spells out its own rules instead of deferring to statutes or courts)?
- Does it include robust funding instructions and mechanisms (deeds, assignments, POD/TOD updates, business entity transfers)?
- Is there a neutral, independent **Trust Protector** with clear powers (remove/replace Trustees, cure ambiguities, adapt to law changes, approve conflicted transactions)?
- Does the Protector's loyalty ultimately align with the Grantor's intent (not the Trustee, Beneficiaries, or politicians)?
- Are Trustee succession provisions forward-looking and multi-generational (Board structure, branch representation, non-family options, incapacity triggers)?
- Is the Trust jurisdiction-independent and portable (can move situs as family/assets move)?
- Does it include integrated components where appropriate:
    - **Family Office** (management/control segregation)
    - **Family Bank** (risk insulation, lending to family members)

- ○ **Family Foundation / Donor-Advised Fund** (capture social capital, charitable influence)
- ○ **Special Purpose Entities** (asset-specific protection/operation)

- Are there principal-protection mechanisms (loans instead of outright distributions, incentives for productivity, addiction/gambling safeguards)?
- Does the Trust allow for future adaptability (legislative/tax ambush recovery, perpetuity provisions, generation-skipping optimization)?
- Have you mapped out your family's wealth and decision-making structures on paper (Trust(s), business entities, Family Office, Family Bank, charitable vehicles)? If not, sketch a simple diagram this week. What gaps appear when you look at it through the lens of 50 or 100 years?
- Does your plan assume today's laws, tax rules, family locations, and investment options will still be favorable decades from now? What single change (new tax law, family move, market shift) could most threaten it, and what adaptability tools are missing?
- Are future generations already being taught how to use the "toolbox" you're building (loans instead of gifts, incentives for productivity, board-style governance)? If not, what is one small way you can begin that education now?
- Have you assembled (or planned to assemble) a true integrated advisory team (attorney, CPA, financial planner, perhaps a family-business consultant) that meets regularly and speaks the same language with a dynasty mindset, and looks beyond simply completing annual tax filings?

AFTER YOU BUILD: ONGOING STEPS TO SUSTAIN THE LEGACY (CHAPTERS 8-10)

- Have you written and shared your **Statements of Wishes** (values, incentives, stories, expectations) with Trustees and family?
- Is there a deliberate **family council** tradition (regular meetings, agenda, opening/closing ceremonies, business discussion, conflict resolution)?
- Have you introduced the next generation to your advisory team (attorney, CPA, financial advisor) and explained their roles?
- Are you modeling self-reliance, modest living, and charitable giving so the next generation learns by example?
- Have you scheduled periodic reviews (every 5-10 years or after major life events) to ensure the Trust remains aligned with changing laws, family needs, and goals?
- Are you actively preparing heirs emotionally and spiritually for inheritance (no surprises, clear expectations, focus on responsibility and purpose)?
- Have you established or funded a **Donor-Advised Fund** or similar structure to redirect inevitable social capital (taxes/ inflation) to causes you value?
- Does your Trust allow assets to **stay inside the Trust** for multiple generations, or do mandatory distributions force them out at set ages, creating windows where creditors, lawsuits, or poor decisions can drain them?
- Does your plan include **discretionary distributions** guided by your Statements of Wishes, so Trustees can say "no" to requests that don't align with your values (education,

entrepreneurship, family unity) while still protecting the principal?

- Are Beneficiaries allowed **beneficial enjoyment** of Trust assets (homes, education, business opportunities) without ever receiving legal title, preserving spendthrift protections and shielding wealth from creditors or claims?
- Have you structured the Trust to favor **loans over outright distributions**? What guidelines in your Statements of Wishes could encourage responsible borrowing and repayment, turning inheritance into a tool for building rather than consuming?
- If GST (Generation-Skipping Transfer) tax exclusion is allocated, are Trust-owned assets explicitly kept out of Beneficiaries' taxable estates? How much could your family preserve tax-free over 50-100 years if the wealth compounds inside the Trust instead of being taxed at each generation?
- Looking at the contrast between the traditional outright-transfer path (losing billions to taxes) and the GST-exempt dynasty path (zero transfer taxes), which future do you want for your descendants? What one change can you make now to move closer to the dynasty model?
- What legacy do you want your family to celebrate, beyond the size of the estate, but the way your Trust keeps wealth working, protected, and purposeful for generations?
- What is one small, realistic step you can take this month to ensure your Trust keeps assets inside, guided by your values, and shielded from unnecessary taxes and risks?
- How much daily time are you currently investing directly in your children and grandchildren (reading, conversations, shared activities) versus outsourcing childcare, tutoring, or enrichment to institutions or professionals? What small,

incremental shift in your schedule could increase that personal presence and model the values you want them to carry forward?

- Does your family have regular, intentional moments (beyond holidays) where you are fully present together, without devices or distractions? Do you eat meals together? Research shows even small daily investments in family time (e.g., 20-30 minutes of focused interaction) can enhance children's emotional regulation, social skills, and long-term mental health. How might you protect or expand those moments starting this week?
- Are family councils being used as a vehicle to give upcoming generations real leadership roles, perhaps letting teens chair a meeting, young adults lead a charitable grant decision, or next-gen members propose Family Bank investment ideas? What would happen if you assigned one upcoming family member a small leadership responsibility in the next council?
- In your family business or Trust-owned enterprises, are younger members given meaningful positions where they can gain hands-on experience, make decisions, and, importantly, learn safely from failure? How could structured roles in these enterprises build their confidence, work ethic, and wealth-creation skills while strengthening collective family resilience?
- If a major financial setback occurred tomorrow (market crash, lawsuit, business failure), would your family have the "wealth mentality" to recover and rebuild, because they've been trained to create value rather than just consume it? What one practice (e.g., family council recovery simulations, Statements of Wishes emphasizing perseverance) could you start now to cultivate that resilience?

- No matter your family's current financial position or the ages of its members, it is never too late to begin investing in people through time, values, and structured opportunities. What is one small step you can take this month to move your family toward a prosperity perspective that thrives on every level: economic, emotional, social, and spiritual?

FINAL REFLECTION

A Dynasty Trust succeeds when the people it serves become stronger, more capable, and more united, not weaker, more entitled, or more divided.

Revisit this checklist regularly. Share it with your advisors and family. The legacy you build is measured not by how much you leave behind, but by who your descendants become because of it.

APPENDIX B

FAMILY COUNCIL AGENDA

SAMPLE FAMILY COUNCIL AGENDA

A Flexible Template for Any Meeting – With Dynasty Planning Focus Options

Family councils are the heartbeat of a thriving multi-generational family. They can be casual Sunday dinners or structured quarterly sessions; both work. The key is consistency, participation, and intentionality. Use this agenda as a starting template. Adapt it to your family's culture, size, and current needs.

When your family is ready to discuss estate planning, legacy, or the tools in this book, simply emphasize or expand the **Dynasty & Legacy Focus** options in the agenda. These prompts help turn ordinary meetings into powerful conversations about wealth, responsibility, and long-term family strength.

OPENING (5-10 MINUTES)

- Welcome & Attendance. Quick round-robin: name, one high point from the past week/month
- Opening Tradition. Choose one your family loves (family motto recitation, short prayer/meditation, favorite song verse, gratitude circle, inspirational quote)

- Set Ground Rules. Remind everyone: respect, no interruptions, speak from the heart, confidentiality within the family

CELEBRATIONS & UPDATES (10-15 MINUTES)

- Recognize milestones: Birthdays, anniversaries, graduations, new jobs, personal achievements
- Quick life updates: Each person shares 1-2 sentences: What's going well? What's challenging?

EDUCATION / TEACHING MOMENT (10-20 MINUTES)

- Assigned topic or presenter. Rotate this role (even children can share something they learned). Examples: book insight, article, podcast, life lesson, financial concept, character trait

Dynasty & Legacy Focus options:

- Share one line from your Statements of Wishes (or read a short section)
- Discuss a principle from the book (e.g., "Dependency breeds contempt" – what does self-reliance look like in our family?)
- Review one "Does It Matter?" question from a chapter

FAMILY BUSINESS & DECISIONS (15-30 MINUTES)

- Old business. Review action items from last meeting (who did what?)
- New business. Current decisions or topics needing family input. Examples: vacation planning, household rules, charitable causes, education choices

Dynasty & Legacy Focus options:

- Review current Trust status: Is everything funded? Any recent life changes requiring updates?

- Discuss Successor Trustees or Protector: Who should we consider? Why?
- Talk about incentives: How can we encourage education, work ethic, or charitable giving?
- Brainstorm Family Bank ideas: What future loans or investments could help family members build their own wealth?
- Charitable/social capital: Are we capturing tax-advantaged giving through a DAF or foundation?

OPEN FORUM / CONFLICT RESOLUTION (10-20 MINUTES ONLY IF NEEDED)

- Safe space to raise concerns. Use "I feel..." statements, focus on solutions
- If conflict arises: pause, breathe, restate the other person's view before responding

CLOSING (5-10 MINUTES)

- Action items recap. Who will do what by when? (Assign owners & deadlines)
- Closing Tradition. Same as opening (or a blessing, group hug, cheer, song)
- Set next meeting date/time. Keep momentum alive

QUICK TIPS FOR SUCCESS

- Rotate who runs the meeting (builds leadership skills in everyone)
- Keep it positive and forward-looking. Focus on possibilities, not blame
- Start small: 30-45 minutes is fine at first

- Document lightly: minutes/action list (one person takes notes)
- When focusing on dynasty planning: bring this book, your Trust summary, or Statements of Wishes to reference

The family that councils together stays strong together. Whether today's topic is dinner plans or a 100-year legacy, every meeting builds the muscle of unity, responsibility, and shared purpose.

Use this agenda regularly. Over time, your family council will become the most valuable "board meeting" any of you ever attend.

APPENDIX C

GLOSSARY

GLOSSARY OF KEY TERMS

This glossary provides clear, concise definitions of the most important concepts used throughout the book. It is designed for quick reference, whether you are a family member reading for the first time or an advisor reviewing with a client. Terms are listed alphabetically.

BENEFICIAL ENJOYMENT

The right of a Beneficiary to use or enjoy Trust-owned assets (e.g., living in a Trust-owned home, driving a Trust-owned vehicle, or accessing Trust-funded education) without holding legal title or ownership. This structure preserves spendthrift protections because creditors or claimants generally cannot reach assets the Beneficiary does not legally own.

DAF (DONOR ADVISED FUND)

A charitable giving vehicle that allows donors to make irrevocable contributions to a sponsoring organization, receive an immediate tax deduction, and retain advisory privileges over how the funds are granted to charities over time. DAFs are a powerful tool for capturing social capital (wealth that would otherwise be lost to taxes) while involving family members in philanthropic decision-making and training. A DAF is a simple low-cost type of Family Foundation distinct from a private foundation.

DISCRETIONARY DISTRIBUTIONS

Distributions of income or principal from a Trust that are made at the Trustee's judgment ("as the Trustee deems advisable") rather than on a mandatory schedule or formula. This flexibility protects assets from creditors (since Beneficiaries have no enforceable right to compel distribution of funds) and allows Trustees to align payouts with the Grantor's values as expressed in Statements of Wishes.

DYNASTY TRUST

A Trust (revocable or irrevocable) designed to last for multiple generations (often in perpetuity where allowed by law), holding and managing assets to provide for descendants while protecting them from taxes, creditors, divorce claims, and poor decision-making. Unlike traditional Revocable Trusts, Dynasty Trusts emphasize asset retention, adaptability, and multi-generational stewardship.

FAMILY BANK

A family-owned entity (often structured as an LLC or limited partnership owned by multiple Trusts) to own cross generational assets and function as an internal investment and lending source, providing loans to family members for homes, businesses, or education rather than outright distributions. Loans preserve Trust principal, teach financial responsibility, and return capital (with interest) for future generations.

FAMILY COUNCIL

A regular, intentional family meeting where members discuss life updates, celebrate milestones, resolve conflicts, make decisions, and address business or legacy topics. Family councils build trust, communication, leadership skills, and shared purpose, all of which are essential human capital that no legal document can create alone.

FAMILY FOUNDATION

A Family Foundation is a private charitable entity funded by the Trust to make grants and engage in philanthropy. In addition to giving back and making the world a better place, a Family Foundation can provide training grounds for the next generation in governance, stewardship, and impact. A Family Foundation may consist of a standalone private foundation or a less expensive and simpler DAF.

FAMILY OFFICE.

A family office is a management structure (often a separate LLC taxed as a C corporation) owned by one or more Trusts that has protected control and oversees investments, administration, and coordination of family wealth and enterprises. It often employs family members both for operational efficiency and for next generation trining.

GST EXCLUSION / GENERATION-SKIPPING TRANSFER TAX EXCLUSION

A federal tax provision allowing a certain amount of assets (the GST exemption, indexed for inflation) to be placed in Trust without incurring generation-skipping transfer tax at each generational level. When allocated at creation, GST-exempt Trust assets are excluded from Beneficiaries' taxable estates, enabling estate tax-free compounding across generations.

INFINITE GAME

A mindset introduced by James P. Carse and applied here to estate planning: unlike the finite game of conventional planning (divide assets, pay taxes, hope for the best), the infinite game has no fixed end. The objective is not to simply win once, but to keep the game going, adapting, growing, and strengthening family and wealth indefinitely through deliberate design, adaptability, and shared purpose.

INTEGRATED DYNASTY TRUST

A comprehensive, multi-generational Trust system that combines legal structures (revocable Dynasty Trust, irrevocable Dynasty Trust, GST exemption), business entities (Family Office, Family Bank, Special Purpose Entities), charitable vehicles (DAF/foundation), and family governance (councils, Statements of Wishes), with an advisory team that buys into and understands the vision, to protect people, grow wealth, and sustain legacy across centuries.

LOANS VS. OUTRIGHT DISTRIBUTIONS

A planning choice where a Trust provides capital to Beneficiaries as loans (with interest, repayment terms, and collateral) rather than outright gifts or distributions. Loans preserve Trust principal, encourage accountability, return funds for future use, and maintain spendthrift protections, turning inheritance into a tool for building rather than consuming.

MANDATORY DISTRIBUTIONS

Trust provisions that require the Trustee to distribute income or principal at fixed ages, events, or intervals (e.g., one-third at age 30, half at 35, remainder at 40) or upon demand by the Beneficiary. While intended to encourage maturity, mandatory payouts often override spendthrift protections, expose assets to creditors, lawsuits, or poor decisions, and can sabotage long-term dynasty goals such as GST planning and wealth preservation.

PRINCIPAL PROTECTION

Mechanisms within a Trust that safeguard the core capital (principal) from depletion, including discretionary distributions, loans instead of gifts, spendthrift clauses, beneficial enjoyment rules, and restrictions on mandatory payouts. The goal is to keep assets inside the Trust so they can compound and serve future generations.

SCOPES OF DISCRETION

A practical ceiling, cap or limit on distributions from a Dynasty Trust in order to protect and grow the assets in the Trust while giving Beneficiaries enough but not too much. Distributions may be limited to income only, or a percentage, or a dollar amount, or a fraction of income with an annual dollar cap adjusted for inflation. Such distributions supplement other Trust benefits such as the ability to use and enjoy Trust assets and access to capital through secured loans.

SELF-GOVERNING TRUST

A Trust that operates primarily by its own private contractual rules (as set by the Grantor) rather than relying heavily on state statutes, court intervention, or default laws. Self-governing Trusts spell out detailed procedures for interpretation, amendment, Trustee succession, and dispute resolution to minimize external control.

SPENDTHRIFT PROVISIONS / SPENDTHRIFT CLAUSE

Language in a Trust that prevents a Beneficiary from voluntarily or involuntarily transferring their interest (e.g., assigning it to creditors or in divorce proceedings) and restricts creditors from reaching Trust assets. These clauses are most effective when distributions remain discretionary and assets stay inside the Trust.

STATEMENTS OF WISHES

Non-binding, precatory guidance from the Grantor (or later family members) that expresses values, principles, incentives, and expectations for how the Trust should be administered. While not legally enforceable, Statements of Wishes guide Trustee discretion, shape distributions/loans/enjoyment, and help align decisions with the family's moral compass across generations.

TRUST PROTECTOR

A neutral, independent party (often a licensed professional or a committee) named in the Trust with specific powers to oversee and adapt the Trust, e.g., remove/replace Trustees, cure ambiguities, modify terms for changed laws, approve conflicted transactions, or resolve disputes. The Protector acts as a check and balance to ensure the Grantor's intent endures without court involvement.

TRUST SITUS / JURISDICTION INDEPENDENCE

The legal "home" of the Trust (governed by the laws of a particular state or jurisdiction). A portable, jurisdiction-independent Trust includes provisions allowing the situs to move as family members, assets, or laws change, avoiding obsolescence and enabling the Trust to operate in the most favorable legal environment over time.

RICHARD E. DURFEE, JR.

Richard E. Durfee Jr. ("Rick") is the principal and founder of Durfee Law Group, PLLC, and has been practicing law since 1988. Although his firm provides a full range of services in estate planning, tax planning, asset protection, business succession, charitable planning, and probate, his personal practice is limited to planning for wealthy individuals and their businesses, focusing on sophisticated, multi-generational strategies and turning the gift of wealth into a blessing rather than a curse. Before founding Durfee Law Group, he helped teach classes on world religions at Arizona State University while pursuing graduate studies. Holding a Bachelor of Arts in Asian Languages (Japanese and Chinese) and a Master of Arts in Religious Studies, his academic background significantly shaped his legal philosophy. This blend of humanities and law informs his client-centered, holistic approach, which prioritizes family harmony and long-term legacy over purely material outcomes. He has pioneered the use of innovations such as Legal Architecture for diagramming complex structures and Integrated Planning to empower clients to obtain the right planning pieces, all working together. Rick has authored many articles and publications and he is a regular speaker at national events like the Money Show, FreedomFest and training events for financial service providers. His goal is to empower his clients to "Live Well, Leave a Legacy."™

Your feedback on this book is welcome and appreciated. Learn more here:

Contact Information:

480.324.8000

Info@DurfeeLawGroup.com

www.DurfeeLawGroup.com

1423 S. Higley Rd. Ste. 127
Mesa, Arizona 85206

Subscribe to Learn More on our YouTube Channel!

www.ingramcontent.com/pod-product-compliance
Lightning Source LLC
Chambersburg PA
CBHW041302210926
51847CB00010B/111
9781971310237